D0384701

SILVER BURDETT
SCIENCE

Centennial Edition

GEORGE G. MALLINSON
Distinguished Professor
of Science Education
Western Michigan University

JACQUELINE B. MALLINSON
Associate Professor of Science
Western Michigan University

WILLIAM L. SMALLWOOD
Head, Science Department
The Community School
Sun Valley, Idaho

CATHERINE VALENTINO
Former Director of Instruction
North Kingstown School Department
North Kingstown, Rhode Island

SILVER BURDETT COMPANY
MORRISTOWN, NJ
Atlanta, GA • Cincinnati, OH • Dallas, TX • Northfield, IL •
San Carlos, CA • Agincourt, Ontario

SILVER BURDETT
SCIENCE

Centennial Edition

GEORGE G. MALLINSON

JACQUELINE B. MALLINSON

WILLIAM L. SMALLWOOD

CATHERINE VALENTINO

THE SILVER BURDETT ELEMENTARY SCIENCE PROGRAM
1-6 PUPILS' BOOKS
AND
TEACHERS' EDITIONS LEVELS K-6

ISBN 0-382-13104-5

CONTENTS

UNIT ONE

Observing Plants and Animals

You may think that plants are very different from animals. In some ways they are. But plants and animals are also much alike. All living things are alike in some ways. Do you know how?

Look at the pictures. Can you tell the plants from the animals? In what ways are these plants and animals alike? In what ways are they different?

In this unit you will study plants and animals. You will find out what they need to live. You will also find out how they are alike, yet different.

Chapter 1

Animals

There are many kinds of animals. Some live on land. Others live in water. Most animals move around. Some walk, some crawl, some fly, and some swim. A few hardly move at all.

What kinds of animals did you see today? Were they all the same size? The same age? Did you see any animals with their young?

All animals produce more of their own kind. What would happen if they did not? In this chapter you will learn about animals and their young. You will find out how the young grow and change.

— ANIMALS AND THEIR YOUNG —
How do animals produce young?

grasshopper

fish

bird

snake

You probably have seen chicken eggs many times. But have you ever seen turtle eggs? Or the eggs of a grasshopper? Turtles, grasshoppers, and many other animals lay eggs. What animals do you know that lay eggs?

Snapping turtle laying an egg

Most animals come from eggs. The eggs are produced by the female animals. The number of eggs produced by each kind of animal is different. Some birds lay only one egg a year, but most birds lay several.

toad

Another animal, the toad, lays up to 6,000 eggs at a time. An oyster (ois'tər), however, may lay as many as 500 million eggs at a time.

An egg contains everything needed to form a new animal. Look closely at these frog eggs. Can you see the new animal forming in each egg?

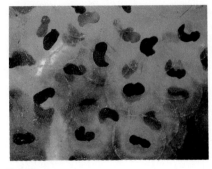

Frog eggs

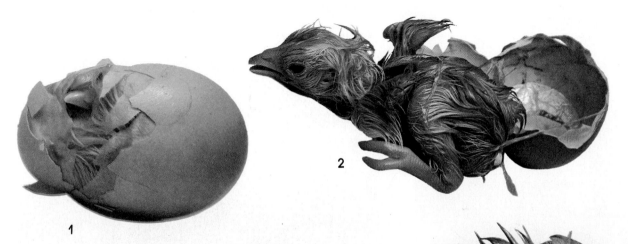

Many eggs have a shell or other covering. The covering keeps the egg from drying out. It also protects the new animal growing inside. Bird eggs have a hard shell. Turtle eggs have a softer shell that is like leather. Frog and snail eggs have a jellylike covering.

When the animal has grown enough, it breaks out of the egg. This is called hatching. Here you can see how a chicken hatches.

Western garter snake and young

Some animals do not lay eggs. Instead, the eggs hatch inside the female's body. After hatching, the live young pass out of her body. Guppies (gup'ēz), most sharks, and some snakes produce young this way.

Other animals also give birth to living young. But these young do not hatch from eggs. They grow in a special way in the female's body. When the young are born, the mother produces milk to feed them. Cows, dogs, and most other mammals (mam'əls) produce young this way. A **mammal** is an animal that has hair and feeds its young with mother's milk.

Cow and newborn calf

Mother pigs feeding young

What can you learn about a chicken egg?

Materials   hand lens / cold hard-cooked egg / uncooked egg / dish / dinner knife

Procedure

A. Tap both ends of the hard-cooked egg against a hard surface. Carefully peel away the shell. Look for an air space at one of the ends of the egg. Examine a piece of the shell with a hand lens.

   1. How were you able to identify the air space?

   2. Describe the shell. What is its purpose?

   3. Is there a thin lining inside the shell? What is its purpose?

B. Cut open the hard-cooked egg. Examine it closely.

   4. Describe what you observe.

C. Carefully open an uncooked egg into a dish. Compare the drawing to the egg.

   5. Point to the parts of egg you can identify.

D. Find the twisted strands of egg white. They hold the yolk in place.

   6. What would happen if the strand broke?

E. Identify the white spot on the yolk. This is the spot from which a baby chicken would grow.

   7. Where does the baby chicken get food?

F. Compare the egg white to the egg yolk.

   8. Describe how they are different.

Conclusion

1. What are the parts of a chicken egg?

2. What does the egg provide for the new animal that may grow inside it?

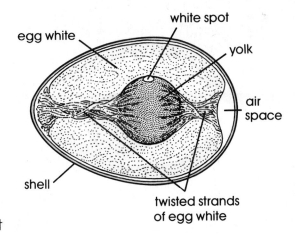

egg white / white spot / yolk / air space / shell / twisted strands of egg white

7

-ANIMALS GROW AND CHANGE -
How do certain animals change as they grow?

Many young animals look much like their parents. Others do not. Some go through stages of growth. In each stage of growth they become more like their parents. Look at the pictures below. Notice how the frog changes in each stage of growth. How does the adult frog differ from the young frog in the first picture? How are they the same?

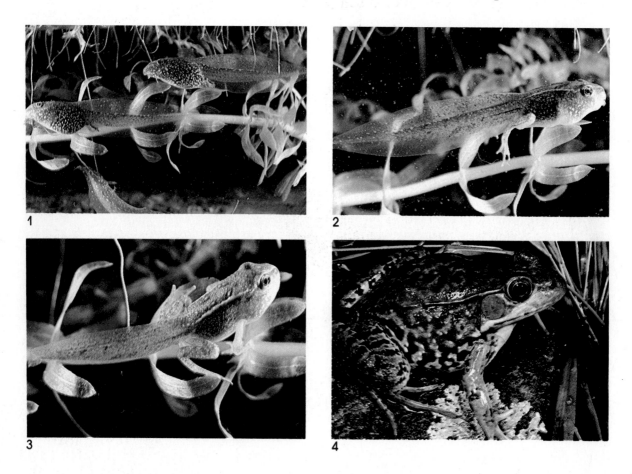

1

2

3

4

Insects also change as they grow. Many go through four stages of growth. Those stages are (1) egg, (2) larva (lär′və), (3) pupa (pyü′pə), and (4) adult. Some insects that change this way are butterflies, moths, and beetles.

Butterfly eggs hatching

The **egg** is the first stage of growth. Insect eggs may be laid almost anywhere. Often they are on leaves or other food the insects can eat after they hatch.

After hatching, the young insect is called a **larva**. A larva is in the second stage of growth. A larva is always hungry. This larva is eating a leaf.

Gypsy moth pupa

Moth larva

After a certain time, a larva stops eating. Then it makes a covering for itself. The covering is usually hard. Now the insect is called a **pupa.** A pupa is in the third stage of growth.

9

Monarch butterfly

Inside the covering, the pupa slowly changes. When the changes are complete, the **adult** insect comes out. This is the fourth stage of growth. Now the insect looks the same as other adults of its kind.

The butterfly in the picture is a new adult. Only a few moments earlier it was a pupa. The butterfly is resting on the covering that it had as a pupa. When its wings are dry, the butterfly will fly away.

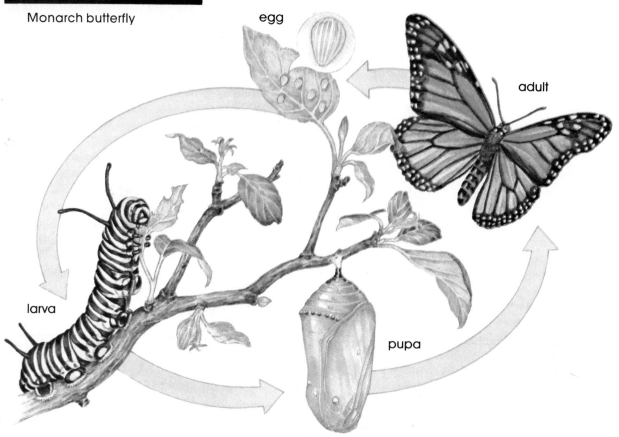

egg

adult

larva

pupa

BUTTERFLY STAGES OF GROWTH

Grasshopper nymph

egg

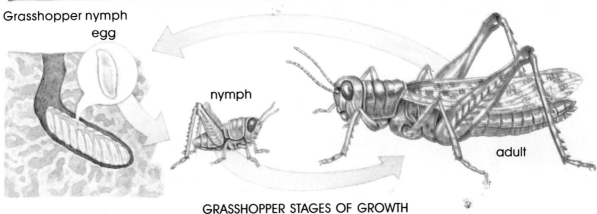

nymph

adult

GRASSHOPPER STAGES OF GROWTH

Some insects, such as grasshoppers, have only three stages of growth. They are (1) egg, (2) nymph (nimf), and (3) adult. After hatching, the young insect is called a **nymph.** A nymph is like a tiny adult. But it does not have wings. The nymph becomes an adult insect when it has wings and can fly.

How does a mealworm change as it grows?

Materials jar / dry cereal / 5 to 10 mealworms / paper towels / piece of cloth / rubber band

Procedure

A. Half fill a jar with dry cereal. Then put 5 to 10 mealworms in the jar.
  1. In what stage of growth is a mealworm?
  2. What will the next stage of growth be?
  3. What do you think the cereal will be used for?

B. Wet a paper towel, and squeeze out most of the water. Lay the towel on the cereal in the jar.
  4. What do you think the mealworms will get from the paper towel?

C. Cover the jar with a piece of cloth. Use a rubber band to hold the cloth in place.

D. Keep the jar in a warm, dry place. Clean the jar every few days. Each time give the mealworms fresh cereal and a new paper towel.

E. Watch for changes to take place as the mealworms grow. Write the changes you see in a chart like the one shown. Describe how the animals look and act in each stage of growth.

Conclusion

1. Was there a stage of growth that you did not see? Which one?
2. In what ways does a mealworm change during each stage of growth?
3. What kind of insect is a mealworm?

Date	Stage	Description

— CARING FOR THE YOUNG —

How do animal parents care for their young?

Some young animals can take care of themselves right away. They do not need parents to help them. Most fish are on their own as soon as they hatch. Newly hatched turtles can walk and eat like adults.

Do you know?

Many fish lay their eggs and leave them. But some fish are caring parents. The female sea horse lays about 200 eggs. Then the male sea horse hatches them. He keeps the eggs in a pouch on the underside of his body.

The ocean catfish puts its eggs in its mouth. They are carried there until the eggs hatch. Often it is the male that carries the eggs this way.

Male sea horse with eggs

Robin feeding young

Lioness carrying her cub

Other young animals cannot live on their own. They must be cared for by one or both parents. Most birds are like that. These robins would die if they were not fed. Why? How else must they be cared for?

Mammals also need care after they are born. What is the special way all mammals are cared for?

Many newborn mammals are helpless. Some, such as bear cubs, are born blind and without hair. Some, such as puppies and kittens, cannot stand up by themselves. But a deer or a bison (bīs' ən) is different. It can see right away. It can stand up within minutes after it is born. After about an hour, it can follow its mother wherever she goes.

Dog feeding puppies

Bison with newborn calf

Finding out

How does a kangaroo care for its young? A kangaroo is one of a special group of mammals. These mammals care for their young in a way that is different from other mammals.

Read about the kangaroo in books about animals. Find out how a young kangaroo is cared for. Also find out what other animals care for their young in this same way. What name is given to this special group of mammals?

Young mammals need more than food. They must be protected from animals that can harm them. Also, some mammals need special skills to live on their own. The young learn those skills by watching their parents. What skill are these bear cubs learning?

Alaskan brown bear with cubs

Mammals need less care as they grow older and stronger. These lion cubs are hunting their own food. Soon they will be able to live on their own. They will not need to be cared for by their parents.

Lion cubs hunting

IDEAS TO REMEMBER

► Most animals come from eggs.
► Some animals produce young from eggs hatched inside the female's body.
► Most mammals give birth to living young.
► Many insects go through four stages of growth—egg, larva, pupa, and adult.
► Some young animals can live on their own. Others must be cared for by parents.

Reviewing the Chapter

SCIENCE WORDS

A. Use all the terms below to complete the sentences.

pupa   egg   adult   nymph   larva

Some young animals look much like their parents. Others do not. Many insects go through four stages of growth before they look like their parents. The first stage is the __1__. After hatching, the young insect is called a __2__. Later, the young insect makes a covering for itself. Now it is called a __3__. Changes take place inside the covering. When the changes are complete, the __4__ insect comes out. Some insects, such as the grasshopper, have only three stages of growth. They are the egg, the __5__, and the adult stages.

B. Unscramble each group of letters to find a science term from the chapter. Write a sentence using each term.

1. cisnet   **2.** mlmama   **3.** thcah

UNDERSTANDING IDEAS

A. Write the letter of the animal that best matches each statement.

1. Its eggs hatch inside the female's body.
2. It lays hard-shelled eggs.
3. It lays jellylike eggs.
4. It has three growth stages.
5. It has hair and gets milk from its mother.

    a. grasshopper
    b. mammal
    c. bird
    d. guppy
    e. frog

B. The drawings show the stages of growth of a moth. Write the numbers of the drawings to show the correct order.

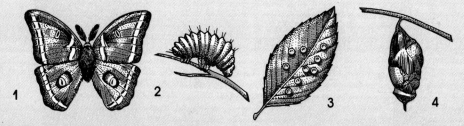

C. Some animals have many young. Others have very few. Which animals do you think would give the best care to their young? Give reasons for your answer.

USING IDEAS

1. Walk around your neighborhood. List the animals you see. Which of those animals lay eggs? Which give birth to living young?

Chapter 2

Animals Are Important

Which animal, do you think, is most important to people? No one can say for sure. Almost all animals are important to people in some way. People keep animals as pets. People also use many things that come from animals.

The picture shows an animal that is useful to people. Years ago, many whales like this one swam in the oceans. Today there are fewer whales. What do you think happened to the whales?

In this chapter you will learn why animals are important to people. You will also learn why some animals must be protected.

FOODS FROM ANIMALS

Which foods come from animals?

Many of the things you use each day come from animals. You may eat foods that come from animals. Many things you wear come from animals. Without animals, there are many things you would not have.

Milking cows

Pig farm

Shopping for meat

You probably drink milk every day. Milk is an important food that comes from cows. Milk can be used to make butter and cheese. Cattle are raised for their meat. The meat from cattle is called beef.

People eat the meat of other animals, too. The meat from a pig is called pork. Ham and bacon also come from a pig. The meat from chickens, turkeys, and ducks is also eaten.

Birds that are used for food are called **poultry** (pōl′trē). What other food comes from poultry?

Cattle, pigs, and birds are raised by people. Some other animals used for food are not raised by people. Many of these animals live in oceans, rivers, and streams. These animals are wild and must be caught.

Have you ever eaten tuna or salmon (sam′ən)? Tuna and salmon are fish. Most tuna and salmon live in the salt water of oceans. Large nets are used to catch these fish. Here you can see that many fish are caught at one time.

Collecting eggs

Ocean fishing

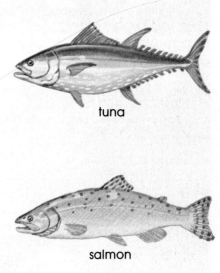

tuna

salmon

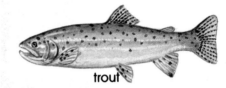
trout

bass

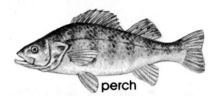
perch

Fishing in fresh water

Other kinds of fish are caught in the fresh water of rivers, lakes, and streams. Some of these fish are bass, trout, and perch. In some places, fish is a very important food.

Do you know?

Without the work of bees there would be no honey. Honeybees take sweet nectar (nek'tər) from flowers. They carry it to their hive. In the hive, the nectar slowly changes from a watery liquid to a thick liquid. This thick liquid is honey.

Not all honey is the same. The flavor and color of honey depend on the kind of flower the nectar came from.

Honeybee on a dandelion

—PEOPLE RAISE OTHER ANIMALS—
Which useful animals do people raise?

Many useful things come from animals. Perhaps you have used some of them. Have you ever slept on a pillow stuffed with feathers? The soft feathers found in most pillows come from ducks and geese. These feathers are called **down**. Down is also used in coats and sleeping bags.

Wool is another useful thing that comes from animals. The hair of a sheep is called wool. In the picture, you can see how wool is cut from a sheep. This wool may be used to

Down-filled jacket

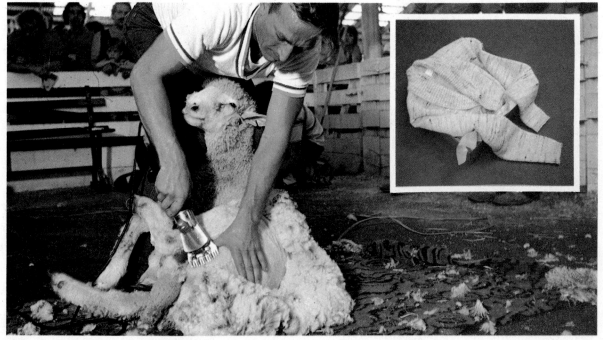
Sheepshearing and wool sweater

25

make clothing and blankets. Many things made from wool are warm and soft.

Some animal skins are also useful. The skins of cattle, sheep, and pigs are called **hides.** Most of these animal hides are used to make leather shoes and leather clothing. Belts, gloves, and footballs can also be made from leather.

Leather objects

Guide dog

If you have a pet, you know another good reason why people need animals. Dogs and cats make good pets. Name some other animals that might make good pets.

Dogs are important to people in other ways. Sometimes dogs are trained to help people who cannot see. Dogs are also trained to protect property.

There are other animals that people depend on. These are animals that can help people to do work. In some places, elephants are used to lift heavy logs. This picture shows how horses help to herd cattle. Horses have also been used to pull loads. Perhaps you can name other animals that help people in some way.

Working elephant

Herding cattle

How has our use of animals changed? Many years ago, people used animals to do a lot of work. Today, machines do much of the work animals used to do.

Read about how animals were used to do work long ago. Make a list of different types of work. Write the name of the animal that was used to do that work. Then write how that work is done today.

How are animals useful to you?

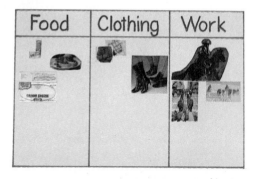

Materials crayons / construction paper / magazine pictures / labels / glue

Procedure

A. Make a chart like the one shown. Make headings for the chart. Write *food* for one heading. Write *clothing* and *work* for each of the other headings.

B. Look for labels on cans, clothing, and other objects showing products that come from animals.

   1. What animals are used for products people use?

C. Paste the labels and the pictures under the correct headings.

   2. Which heading has the most products from animals?

   3. Which kind of products do you think are most important? Give reasons for your answers.

Conclusion

1. Describe ways people use animals.

2. Name things that can be used in place of animal products.

3. Are animals important to people? Tell why.

Using science ideas

How might the use of animals by people cause a problem?

ENDANGERED ANIMALS
Why are some wild animals endangered?

Many wild animals are important for their meat, hides, and other things. This is why people have always hunted these animals.

Many whales used to swim in the oceans. They swam together in large groups. But whales were needed for their fat. This fat, called blubber (blub´ər), was used to make whale oil. The oil was burned in lamps for light. Whales were also important for their meat and bone. Because of this, people hunted and killed whales. More whales were killed than were born. Soon there were very few whales. When only a few animals of a certain kind remain, that kind of animal is **endangered** (en dān´jərd). Now whales are endangered animals.

Humpback whale

Sea turtle

Tortoise

Like the whale, many other kinds of wild animals are endangered. Too many of them have been hunted and killed. Some turtles have been killed for their shells. The shells are used to make jewelry. Wild cats such as tigers and leopards (lep′ərdz) have been

Bengal tiger

Leopard

killed for their fur. Elephants are hunted for
their long white tusks. These tusks are made
of ivory (ī′vər ē). Ivory is used to make
beautiful things. All of these animals are
now endangered.

Some wild animals are endangered for
another reason. People have changed the
places where these wild animals live.
Because of this, the animals do not have
places to raise their young.

Many of the places where elephants live
have been changed. Most elephants live in
grasslands. Grasslands have been changed

African elephant

because people need more land to farm and build houses. Now there are fewer places for elephants to live.

The bald eagle is also an endangered animal. People have cleared many forests where this bird builds its nests. Without places to build nests, the bald eagle cannot produce young. People sometimes use poisons to kill insect pests. The insects are eaten by fish, which are eaten by the eagles. The poisons can then harm the eagles.

Bald eagle at nest and young eagle

What important animal am I?

Materials construction paper / animal picture / glue / hole punch / yarn

Procedure

A. Glue an animal picture on a piece of construction paper. Think of things you may know about the animal.

1. What is the name of the animal?
2. Where does the animal live?
3. What does the animal eat?
4. Is the animal useful to people?
5. Is the animal endangered?
6. Have you ever seen the animal? Where?

B. Use a hole punch to put two holes in the paper.

C. Put a piece of yarn through the holes. Tie the yarn to make a loop.

D. Place the paper in a large box.

E. Someone will pick one of the papers to hang on your back. Try to find out what the animal is. Ask questions about the animal to help you guess its name.

Conclusion

1. Which animals are useful to people?
2. Which animals are endangered?

Using science ideas

How would your life be different if there were no farm animals, no pets, and no wild animals?

ANIMALS NEED PEOPLE

How are endangered animals protected?

This animal is a dodo (dō'dō) bird. You can only see this kind of a bird in a picture. The dodo bird is extinct (ek stingkt'). An animal that is **extinct** is gone forever.

Dodo bird

Here is a condor. There are less than 50 of these birds living. They live in a wildlife refuge (wīld'līf   ref'yüj). A **wildlife refuge** is a place where wild animals are safe. If there were no refuges, many wild animals like the condor would become extinct.

Laws have also been made to protect wild animals. These laws control hunting, fishing,

Condor

and trapping. Some kinds of wild animals may not be hunted or caught at all. Other kinds of animals may be hunted or caught only at certain times. This is to protect some kinds of animals when they are having their young. Laws like this help many endangered animals.

Control of hunting

Safe place for eagles

IDEAS TO REMEMBER

▶ Many useful things come from animals.
▶ People raise some of the animals they use.
▶ Many kinds of wild animals are hunted and killed.
▶ Some kinds of wild animals are endangered.
▶ Many wild animals are being protected.

Reviewing the Chapter

SCIENCE WORDS

A. Use all the terms below to complete the sentences.

poultry   hides   cattle   down   cows

Many things you use each day come from animals. You might drink milk that comes from __1__ and eat beef that comes from __2__. The meat of chickens, turkeys, and ducks is also eaten. Birds that are used for food are called __3__. Other useful things come from animals. Soft feathers from ducks and geese are used to make pillows. These feathers are called __4__. The skins of sheep, pigs, and cattle are also useful. These skins are called __5__.

B. Find the missing letters for each term. Write a sentence using each term.

1. _ n _ a n _ e _ _ d
2. e _ t _ n c _
3. w i l l l i f e r e f u z e

UNDERSTANDING IDEAS

A. Write the letter of the term that goes with the animal. Not all the terms will be used.

1. sheep	**a.** ivory
2. whale	**b.** fur
3. cattle	**c.** bacon
4. elephant	**d.** wool
5. pig	**e.** down
6. leopard	**f.** beef
	g. blubber

B. Make a chart like the one shown. Write the names of animals from the chapter under each heading.

Useful animals people raise	Wild animals people hunt	Endangered animals

C. Tell what would happen if the number of adult bluebirds dying is greater than the number born.

USING IDEAS

1. Make a poster to let people know about an endangered animal.

Chapter 3

Seed Plants

What kinds of plants did you see today? Did any of them look like the plants in the picture? These plants appear to be very different. They have different shapes and sizes. Some are different colors. Although these plants seem to be different, they are alike. They all are seed plants. Why, do you think, are they called seed plants?

Most seed plants have the same plant parts. The parts may not always look the same in all plants, but they do the same jobs.

In this chapter you will learn about seed plants. You will learn about their roots, stems, leaves, and other parts.

ROOTS
What do roots do?

Have you ever tried to pull out weeds in a garden? Did they come out easily? Weeds and most other seed plants have roots that grow in the ground. In some plants, the roots may grow more than 6 meters deep. Roots hold plants in place. Look at these trees. Even a strong wind usually cannot blow them over.

What else do roots do? Roots take in the water and minerals (min′ər əls) plants need.

Palm trees in a storm

Plants need minerals to grow and to be healthy. The water and minerals are carried in tiny tubes in the roots to the stem.

In some plants, food is stored in the roots. Have you ever eaten a carrot, radish, or beet? If so, you have eaten a root with stored food.

Different kinds of plants have different kinds of roots. Some plants have one large main root and other smaller roots. The large main root is called a **taproot.** Other plants have many roots that are all about the same size. These roots are **fibrous** (fī′brəs) **roots.** Look at the drawing. Which plants have fibrous roots? Which plants have a taproot?

dandelion   wheat   beet   cattail

41

Another kind of root is the prop root. **Prop roots** are extra roots that grow out from the sides of stems. On some trees they grow downward from the tree branches. Corn plants and mangrove (mang'grōv) trees have prop roots. How do you think prop roots got that name?

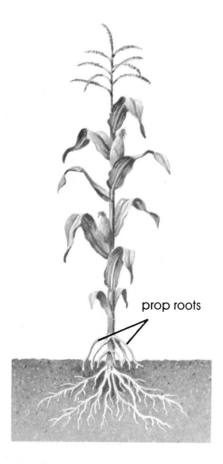

prop roots

Mangrove trees

Finding out

Does more of a plant grow in the ground, or above the ground? Get a potted plant. Take the plant out of the pot. Wash the soil off the roots with water. Then lay the plant on newspaper and carefully spread the roots and leaves.

Draw a circle around the roots. Draw another circle around the part of the plant that was above the ground. Cut along the lines you drew.

Compare the sizes of the two circles. Which circle is larger? Does more of this plant grow in the ground, or above the ground?

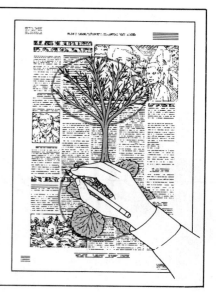

STEMS
What do stems do?

The stems of most plants grow above the ground. They support, or hold up, the leaves, flowers, and other plant parts. Usually stems grow upward. But strawberries and some other plants have stems that grow along the ground. In still other plants, part of the stem grows underground. A potato is a stem that grows underground.

Strawberries

Zinnias

Potatoes

As you know, plants need water and minerals. These materials are taken in by the roots and are carried to the stem. Stems have tiny tubes like those in roots. Water and minerals are carried in those tubes to all parts of the plant. Look at the pictures. How do they show that stems carry materials to another part of the plant? The red, white, and blue flower was all white, like the one at the left. But its stem was split into three parts. Each part carried water of a different color to the flower.

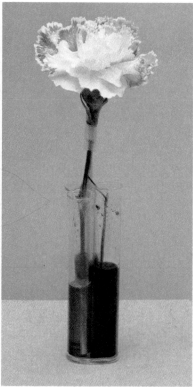

There are four main kinds of seed plants. They are (1) trees, (2) shrubs, (3) herbs (ėrbz), and (4) vines. Each has a different kind of stem.

Most **trees** have one main stem called a trunk. The trunk is a woody stem. It is stiff and hard and covered with bark. Maples, oaks, and pines are common types of trees.

A **shrub** is smaller than a tree and has many woody stems. Some shrubs are called bushes. Rosebushes and lilac (lī'lǝk) bushes are types of shrubs.

Pine tree

French lilac bush

Sugar maple tree

45

Field of grass

Goldenrod in field of wild flowers

Trout lily

An **herb** is another kind of seed plant. Herbs are small plants with soft rather than woody stems. Many herbs die at the end of one growing season. Grasses, flowers, and most weeds are types of herbs. Goldenrod is a weed that is an herb.

Many different herbs are used as food. Some people even have herb gardens. Have you ever eaten herbs such as parsley (pärs'lē) or chives (chīvz)?

Pumpkin

English ivy

A **vine** is another kind of plant with a soft stem. Vines cannot stand by themselves. They climb by wrapping around other things or they creep along the ground. Cucumber, pumpkin, and ivy are vines.

Do you know?

Bamboo (bam bü') is a grass that can grow as tall as a tree. But it has a hollow stem. Some stems may be more than 20 centimeters across. Bamboo grows very quickly. One kind grows more than 2 centimeters in an hour.

Bamboo is used in many ways. The seeds, leaves, and young plants are used as food. The stems are used to make such things as furniture, paper, and baskets.

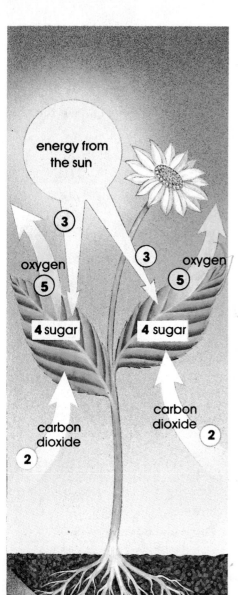

energy from
the sun

3

oxygen
5

4 sugar

carbon
dioxide
2

oxygen
5

4 sugar

carbon
dioxide
2

3

1 water

LEAVES

What do leaves do?

Green plants make their own food. Most of the food is made in the leaves of plants. The leaves of plants can be compared to a factory. Things must be brought to a factory before a product can be made. What things does a factory need? What brings these things to a factory?

A leaf also needs certain things before food can be made. Look at the drawing. (1) One thing the leaf needs is water. Water is brought in through the roots and carried by stems to the leaf. (2) A leaf also needs a gas called carbon dioxide (kär'bən   dī ok'sīd). Carbon dioxide enters the leaf through small openings on the surface of the leaf. (3) Both the leaf and a factory need energy. A factory gets energy by burning coal or other fuels. A leaf gets energy from the sun. (4) The food made by plants is sugar. Plants use the food they make to live and grow. How do you use food made by plants? A plant also makes a gas called oxygen (ok'sə jən). Oxygen is needed by most living things to stay alive. It is released into the air by green plants.

Banana plant

Juniper

American elm tree

Palm

Some leaves are large, and others are small. Large leaves can make more food than small leaves can make.

Leaves have different shapes. Look at these pictures of leaves. Some are shaped like spines. Some are long and flat with a smooth edge. Still others have a toothlike edge. Some leaves even have a shape like the scales of a fish. People use the shapes of leaves to tell one kind of plant from another. Why do leaves have different shapes?

Saguaro cactus

How are some leaves different from others?

LEAF EDGES

toothed   smooth   lobed

VEIN PATTERNS

X   Y   Z

Materials   leaf from 2 different kinds of plants /
hand lens

Procedure

A. Look at the shape of each leaf. Some
leaves are narrow and some are wide. Some
leaves are short and some are long. Some
leaves are rounded and some have points.
   1.   What is the shape of each of your
        leaves?

B. Use a hand lens to look at the edge of each
leaf. Different kinds of leaves have different
edges. The edges may be smooth, toothed, or
lobed. Compare your leaves with the leaves in
the drawings.
   2.   What kind of edge does each of your
        leaves have?

C. Different leaves have different patterns of
veins. Some leaves have veins that all start at
the stem. Some leaves have one large vein
and many smaller veins. Compare your leaves
with the drawings that show vein patterns.
   3.   Which of these vein patterns does each of
        your leaves have?

D. Draw a picture of each of your leaves. Show
the shape of the leaf, the kind of edge, and
the vein pattern.

Conclusion
In what ways are your two leaves different from
each other?

FLOWERS AND SEEDS
What do flowers and seeds do?

Many green plants are seed plants. Some, such as trees and shrubs, live for many years. Others, such as most herbs, live only one growing season and then die.

Seeds may be formed in different ways. Most seed plants first produce flowers. The flowers form on the stems.

Forsythia

Summer at the pond

Alyssum

Autumn at the pond

Flowering crab tree

51

How apples form

Pea pods

As a flower grows, it slowly changes. After a while the outside parts of the flower dry up and fall off. At the same time, the inside part begins to grow. It changes into a fruit. The seeds form inside the fruit.

When you think of a fruit, you probably think of an apple or a pear. But walnuts, melons, and pea pods are fruits also. Even a milkweed pod is a fruit. What other fruits can you name? You probably have eaten many different fruits. Some fruits are good to eat, but many are not. A fruit such as a milkweed pod should not be eaten.

Have you ever seen trees like those in the pictures? They are seed plants, but they do not produce flowers. They produce cones instead. The seeds form inside the cones. When the cones dry, they open and the seeds fall out.

Seeds in a honeydew melon

Cones on a tree

Dry cone with seeds

53

Each seed has a covering called the **seed coat.** Inside the seed coat is a small plant. The plant has a tiny root, stem, and leaf. There is also stored food in the seed. Find these parts of the seed in the drawing.

Seeds have many different shapes and sizes. But all seeds are alike in one way—they can produce new plants. How are the seeds in the pictures different?

Beggar-ticks

Shagbark hickory nuts

Milkweed pods and seeds

Cottonwood pods and seeds

A seed can produce a new plant only if it germinates (jėr'mə nāts). The seed **germinates** when the tiny plant inside begins to grow. This happens only when conditions are right. What do you think those conditions are? As the tiny plant grows, it uses the stored food in the seed. Later, when the plant has grown leaves, it will make its own food.

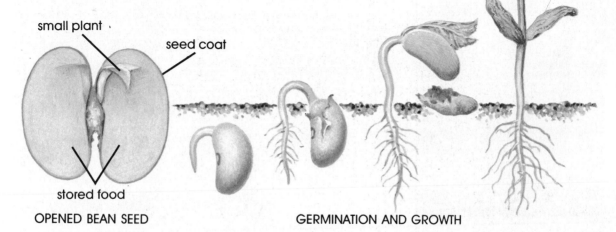

small plant

seed coat

stored food

OPENED BEAN SEED

GERMINATION AND GROWTH

Do seeds germinate at the same time?

Materials   paper towels / small jar / 3 radish seeds / 3 grass seeds / 3 corn seeds

Procedure

A. Fold a paper towel into a strip. The strip should be as wide as the jar is high.

B. Wet the paper towel and place it around the inside of the jar. Then fill the jar with crushed wet paper towels.

C. Carefully put three radish seeds between the jar and the strip of paper towel. In a different place, put three grass seeds between the jar and the towel. In another place, put three corn seeds.

   1. Which seeds do you think will germinate first?

   2. Which seeds do you think will germinate last?

D. Make a chart like the one shown.

E. Look at the jar each day. Keep the paper towels wet. Watch for the seeds to change. Write the changes that you see in your chart.

   3. Why should you keep the paper towels wet?

Conclusion

1. Did the radish seeds all germinate at the same time? Did the grass seeds? Did the corn seeds?

2. Did the three kinds of seeds germinate at the same time?

Date	Radish seeds	Grass seeds	Corn seeds

IDEAS TO REMEMBER

▶ Seed plants are green plants.

▶ Most seed plants have the same plant parts—roots, stems, leaves, flowers, and seeds.

▶ Roots hold a plant in place. They also take in water for the plant.

▶ Stems support the plant parts that grow above the ground. Water and other materials are carried in the stems to other parts of the plant.

▶ Seed plants make their own food. The food is usually made in the leaves.

▶ Seed plants produce seeds from which new plants grow.

Reviewing the Chapter

SCIENCE WORDS

A. Use all the terms below to fill in the blanks.

carbon dioxide   vines   herbs

shrubs   tree   oxygen

There are four main kinds of seed plants. A __1__ has one main woody stem called a trunk. Rosebushes have many woody stems and are called __2__. Plants with soft stems that cannot stand by themselves are called __3__. Plants such as grasses have soft stems also. These plants are called __4__.

All of these plants make their own food in their green leaves. The food is made from water and a gas called __5__. As the leaves make food, they give off a gas called __6__. Most living things need this gas to stay alive.

B. Write the meaning of these terms. Use each term in a sentence.

1. seed coat   **2.** taproot   **3.** germinates

4. fibrous roots   **5.** prop roots

UNDERSTANDING IDEAS

A. Make a chart like the one shown. Write the name of each plant in the correct place in the chart.

pumpkin   lilac bush   maple   cucumber   ivy

pine   goldenrod   grass   rosebush   oak

Trees	Shrubs	Herbs	Vines

B. Use the terms below to label the drawing. Describe what each part does for the plant.

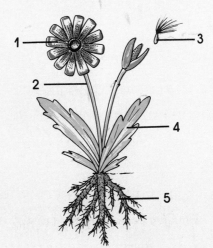

root   stem   leaf

flower   seed

USING IDEAS

1. Get a leaf from a plant that grows outdoors. Tape it to a sheet of paper. Next to the leaf, make a drawing of the plant. Find out what the name of the plant is. Read about the plant's roots, leaves, and other parts. Then write a story that the plant might tell to describe itself.

Chapter 4

Plants Are Important

Think of what the world would be like if there were no plants. Would you have food? Would you have clothing? Would you have a place to live?

Look at the picture. Do you see any plants? Look again. There are many things in the picture that come from plants or parts of plants. Name those that you find.

Of all living things, plants are the most important. In this chapter you will learn why plants are so important. Also, you will find out some ways that plants or parts of plants are used.

FOOD FROM PLANTS

How are plants used as food?

As you know, green plants make their own food. You learned that carbon dioxide and water is changed into sugar in the leaves. Usually more sugar is made than the plant can use. The extra sugar is changed into starch (stärch) and other plant products. **Starch** is the stored food in seeds. It may also be stored in roots, stems, and leaves.

Potatoes

Carrots

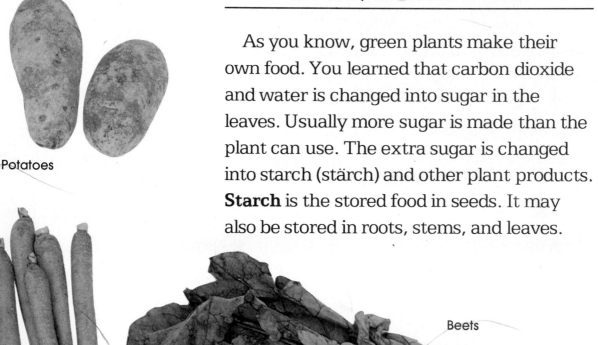

Beets

Peanuts

Lettuce

Green plants are used as food by many living things. Many of the foods you eat are parts of green plants. Cabbage, lettuce, and spinach are plant leaves. Potatoes, rhubarb (rü′bärb), and asparagus (ə spar′ə gəs) are stems. Radishes, beets, and carrots are roots. Peaches, tomatoes, and cucumbers are fruits. Corn, dry beans, and peanuts are seeds. How many of these foods have you eaten? What other leaves, stems, roots, fruits, and seeds are foods?

Corn

Spinach

Tomatoes

Cucumbers

Asparagus

Cabbage

Radishes

63

How can you show there is starch in a green leaf?

Materials   cornstarch / potted plant / alcohol / iodine solution / small beaker / petri dish / pencil / 2 paper towels

Procedure

A. Iodine is used to test for starch. Place some cornstarch on a paper towel. Put a drop of iodine solution on the cornstarch. Caution: Iodine stains and is harmful if swallowed.

   1. What color is the cornstarch?

   2. What color is the cornstarch after you put iodine solution on it?

B. Pick a leaf off a plant. Lay it on a paper towel on your desk. Roll a pencil over the leaf several times. Press hard as you do this.

C. Place the leaf in a beaker. Pour alcohol into the beaker until the leaf is covered. Caution: This kind of alcohol is harmful if swallowed. Let the leaf soak overnight.

D. Take the leaf out of the alcohol and place it in a petri dish.

   3. What color is the alcohol?

   4. What color is the leaf?

   5. Tell what will happen if you cover the leaf with iodine solution.

E. Cover the leaf with iodine solution.

   6. Describe what happens to the leaf.

Conclusion

Is there starch in the green leaf? Where did the starch come from?

Using science ideas

Is there starch in bread or in a potato? How can you find out?

Sometimes you may not recognize a food as being part of a plant. Breakfast foods such as oatmeal and cornflakes are made from seeds. Flour is also made from seeds. These foods are made from seeds called grains (grānz). **Grains** are the seeds of certain grasses such as oats and corn. Wheat and rice are other examples of grains. Many different kinds of grains are used as food by both people and animals.

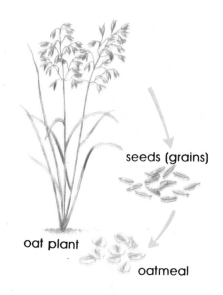

seeds (grains)

oat plant

oatmeal

Wheat field

Rice field

Coffee seeds (beans)

Tea leaves

Cacao seeds and pods

Do you drink cocoa or hot chocolate? Cocoa and chocolate are made from the seeds of the cacao (kə kā′ō) tree. Coffee is also made from the seeds of a certain kind of tree. The leaves of still other kinds of trees are used to make tea.

Seeds, as well as the fruits of some plants, contain oil. Some of those oils are used for cooking. Corn oil is such an oil. What other cooking oils can you name?

Do you use mustard? Mustard is a spice used to flavor foods. Cloves, nutmeg, pepper, and cinnamon (sin′ə mən) are also spices. These and other spices come from plants.

Often a single kind of plant is used as food in different ways. Look at the drawing of the corn plant. What are some of the ways it is used as food?

Most people eat some foods that are not parts of green plants. Do you eat meat and eggs? Do you drink milk? These foods come from animals that eat green plants. Without green plants, there would be no meat, milk, or eggs.

Some plants used for food are not green plants. Look at the pictures. Have you ever eaten plants like these? These plants are mushrooms. Most of the mushrooms that people eat are grown on mushroom farms.

Mushroom

Mushroom factory

How can you tell if a seed or a fruit contains oil?

Materials   brown paper bag / scissors /crayon /
2 toothpicks / water / cooking oil /walnut or
peanut / olive / sunflower seed /orange peel
or lemon peel / apple

Procedure

A. Cut out a large piece from a brown paper
bag. Using a crayon, draw circles on the piece
of brown paper. You will need at least seven
circles.

B. Use a toothpick to put a drop of water in
one circle. Use another toothpick to put a drop
of cooking oil in another circle. Label these
circles *water* and *oil.*

C. In each of the other circles, place a piece
of a fruit or a piece of a crushed seed. Write
the name of the fruit or seed below the circle.

   1. Which of these fruits and seeds do you
      think contain oil?

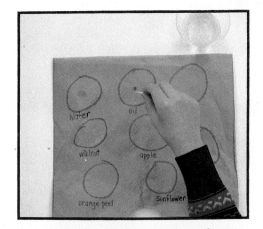

D. Press down hard with your thumb on each
piece of fruit or seed. Press on one piece at a
time. Be sure to wash and dry your fingers
before each test.

E. Take the seeds and fruits off the paper. Wait
for the paper to dry. Then hold it up to a light.

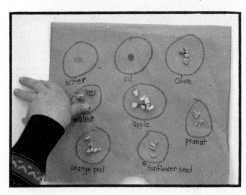

Conclusion

Which fruits and seeds contain oil? How do you
know?

Using science ideas

Do other plant parts contain oil? How can you
find out?

OTHER USES OF PLANTS

How are plants used other than as food?

Bouquet of flowers

You may think that plants are important only as food. But they are also important in other ways.

Plants are often used for decoration. Many people grow house plants because they are pretty or they smell nice. Flowers help to make a room look bright and cheerful.

Plants are also used for decoration outdoors. What kinds of plants are used for decoration in this picture?

Plants for decoration outdoors

Sometimes plants that are grown for decoration are also used in other ways, such as for shade. In some places, rows of trees are used as windbreaks. Other trees and shrubs are used as living fences. Grass and other plants growing on a hillside help to hold the soil in place.

Grass clippings, leaves, and other plant parts can be made into compost (kom'pōst). **Compost** is rotted plant material. When compost is mixed into the soil, it returns minerals to the soil. It also helps to hold water in the soil.

Trees used as a windbreak

Compost pile

Plants used to hold soil

71

Penicillin mold

Many medicines come from plants. Have you ever had to take penicillin (pen ə sil'in)? Penicillin is a medicine made from a certain kind of mold. Oil of wintergreen and castor oil come from other kinds of plants. Many of the medicines used to ease pain are made from plants.

Some plants produce materials that are made into cloth for clothing. You may be wearing some clothing made of cotton. The

Do you know?

Most of the plants from which medicines are made grow wild. They grow in all parts of the world, especially in the tropics. However, an aloe (al'ō) plant is one that some people might grow in their home. The aloe plant has a special juice in its fleshy leaves. When the cut leaves are pressed against the skin, the juice oozes out. The juice is a kind of medicine. It makes the pain of minor cuts and burns go away.

Aloe plant

Cotton plant

Clothing factory

cotton fibers (fī′bərz) that are woven into cloth are produced by the seeds of the cotton plant. Rope and bags are also made from plant fibers. Other plant materials are made into such things as rayon (rā′on) cloth and brooms.

Rope, broom, and canvas bag

Paper products

Charcoal

Tapped rubber tree

Cork products and stripped cork tree

Anything made of wood comes from trees. Many kinds of trees are used for lumber. Paper and charcoal are also made from wood. Rubber, chewing gum, and cork come from trees. Many trees produce oils that are made into waxes and paints. Many dyes (dīz) used to color cloth and to make ink are products of trees.

The ways that plants are used is almost endless. What other uses of plants can you think of?

HARMFUL PLANTS
How are some plants harmful?

Although many plants are useful, some other plants are harmful. Most molds spoil food. You probably have seen mold growing on fruit and other foods.

Another harmful plant is mildew (mil'dü). **Mildew** is a nongreen plant that grows in shady damp places. Often it is found growing on leather, painted surfaces, water pipes, and basement walls. You may have seen it growing in the bathroom around the tub or shower. Like some molds, mildew ruins the things it grows on.

Mold growing on oranges

Mildew growing on leather

Some green plants are harmful, too. These plants may be found growing in the woods and in fields. They also may be found in your home, in your yard, or in a park. Often these plants can cause illness or death if they are eaten. Sometimes only part of a plant is harmful. Sometimes the whole plant may be harmful. Just touching some plants can make your skin blister and itch.

SOME HARMFUL PLANTS YOU SHOULD KNOW

Plant	Harmful part	How it is harmful
Poison ivy	All	Touching
Poinsettia	Leaves, stem, and milky sap	Eating
Yew	All	Eating
Holly	Berries	Eating
Buttercup	All	Eating
Some mushrooms	All	Eating

What does bread mold look like? Sprinkle a few drops of water on a small piece of bread. Then wipe the bread on a dusty floor. Lay the bread with the dusty side up in a plastic sandwich box or margarine tub. Cover the box or tub tightly, and place it in a warm dark place. Mold should grow on the bread in a few days. Look at the mold with a hand lens. What does the bread mold look like? What color is it? What does the mold use for food?

IDEAS TO REMEMBER

▶ Green plants are used as food by many living things.

▶ The roots, stems, leaves, fruits, or seeds of some plants are used for food.

▶ A mushroom is a nongreen plant used for food.

▶ Plants are useful in many ways other than as food.

▶ Among the many things made from plants are lumber, waxes, clothing, and paper.

▶ Some plants are not safe to eat or touch.

Reviewing the Chapter

SCIENCE WORDS

A. Unscramble each group of letters to find a science term from the chapter. Then copy the sentences below. Use one term to complete each sentence.

      1. nagisr   **2.** thacsr   **3.** ptocmso

  4. Rotted plant material is called ___.

  5. Seeds of certain grasses, such as oats and corn, are called ___.

  6. The stored food in seeds is called ___.

B. Write the letter of the term that best matches the definition. Not all the terms will be used.

1. Returns minerals to the soil	**a.** starch
2. Food plants that are not green	**b.** mustard
	c. milk
3. A spice	**d.** mildew
4. A harmful plant often found growing in basements and bathrooms	**e.** mushrooms
	f. compost
5. Seeds used for breakfast foods	**g.** grains
	h. cotton
6. A medicine from a plant	**i.** penicillin
7. A food from some animals	
8. Plant fibers that can be woven into cloth	

UNDERSTANDING IDEAS

A. Describe three uses of plants other than as food.

B. All the foods named below are parts of green plants. Make a chart like the one shown. Write the name of each food in the correct place in the chart.

tomato	cucumber	radish	carrot
lettuce	rhubarb	cocoa	corn
coffee	dry beans	cabbage	peach
spinach	asparagus	peanut	beet

Leaf	Stem	Fruit	Seed	Root

C. Describe three ways plants can be harmful.

USING IDEAS

1. Draw a picture like the one shown. Use crayons to draw plants in your picture. Show how you would use plants for decoration, for a windbreak, for holding soil in place, and for shade. Draw a vegetable garden, too.

Science in Careers

An interest in plants and animals can lead to many kinds of jobs. *Gardeners* plant trees, shrubs, and flowers. They must know which plants will grow best in different places.

Park rangers and *game wardens* protect wild animals from people who could harm them.

Foresters

Foresters care for the trees in forests. They choose the trees that will be cut down and made into lumber and paper. They also fight forest fires and plant new trees.

Botanists (bot'ə nists) are scientists who study plants and plant life. They try to learn new things about plants.

Park ranger

Botanist

People in Science

Jane van Lawick-Goodall

(1934–   )

Jane van Lawick-Goodall is a zoologist (zō ol'ə jist). She studies the behavior of animals such as baboons and chimpanzees. She studies the animals at close range as they live in the wild. She observes what the animals do and how they get along with each other.

Baboons living in the wild

Developing Skills

WORD SKILLS

The important science terms used in this book are listed in the Glossary. The Glossary is found at the back of the book. It gives the meanings of the terms.

Use the Glossary to answer these questions.

1. In what order are the terms in the Glossary listed?
2. What other information is in the Glossary?

There is also an Index at the back of this book. The Index is a list of important topics. Subtopics are listed below the main topic.

Use the Index to answer these questions.

1. In what order are the topics listed?
2. On what pages can you find information about stems?

READING A PICTOGRAPH

A pictograph is an easy way to show information. In a pictograph, pictures are used as symbols. The pictograph on the next page shows how many apples a farmer picked in 5 days. Each apple is a symbol that stands for 10 apples.

Use the graph to answer these questions.

1. How many apples were picked on Tuesday?
2. On which day were the most apples picked?
3. On which day were the fewest apples picked?
4. How many more apples were picked on Monday than on Friday?
5. How many apples were picked during the 5 days?

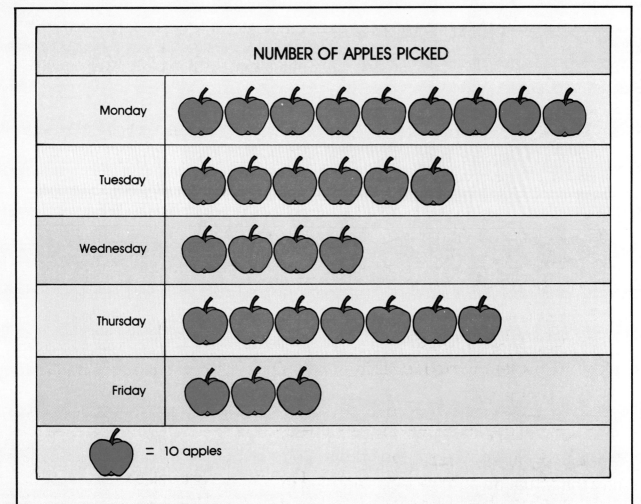

NUMBER OF APPLES PICKED

Monday	🍎🍎🍎🍎🍎🍎🍎🍎🍎
Tuesday	🍎🍎🍎🍎🍎🍎
Wednesday	🍎🍎🍎🍎
Thursday	🍎🍎🍎🍎🍎🍎🍎
Friday	🍎🍎🍎

🍎 = 10 apples

MAKING A PICTOGRAPH

On a chicken farm, eggs are collected each day. Make a pictograph that shows the number of eggs that were collected during 5 days. Use a drawing of an egg, like the one shown, as a symbol. ⬭ Each symbol stands for 5 eggs. Use the information below for your pictograph.

Day	Number of eggs
Monday	25
Tuesday	15
Wednesday	30
Thursday	10
Friday	20

83

UNIT TWO

Observing Matter and Energy

Each of the events shown in the pictures seems to be different from the others. You may think that an auto race has nothing in common with a person raking leaves. The same might be said about a rocket launch and a marching band. Yet these events are alike in several ways. In what ways do you think they are alike?

In this unit you will learn what these events have in common. You will learn that they are alike because of certain things that are happening. You will also learn what is causing those things to happen.

Chapter 5

All About Matter

Putting a model together can be fun. These children are looking for pieces that will fit together. After all the pieces have been put in the right places, they will form a model car.

Do you know that everything around you is made of small pieces? But the pieces are so small that you cannot see them. Like the pieces of the model, they are joined in a special way.

In this chapter you will learn about the small pieces that form the things around you.

PROPERTIES OF MATTER
What is matter?

Look at the objects on the table. You probably use objects like these every day. They look very different from each other. But they are all alike in one way. They are all made of **matter.**

Many kinds of matter

Each object on the table has a different color and size. And each has a different shape. Color, size, and shape are properties (prop'ər tēz). Different properties help you tell these things apart.

The objects on the table have other properties, too. All of them take up space. Which object takes up the most space? Which one takes up the least space?

The objects on the table are different in another way. Some are heavier than others. They have more mass. **Mass** is the measure of how much matter there is in an object.

All matter takes up space and has mass. If you look around, you will see many kinds of matter. You yourself take up space and have mass. So you are made of matter, too.

Sometimes you can see how much space matter takes up. But you cannot see how much mass it has. These children are finding the mass of a book. To do this, they are using a balance (bal'əns). A **balance** is a tool that is used to measure mass.

Measuring mass

What are some properties of matter?

Materials   a box of assorted objects

Procedure

A. Look at the objects in the box. They are all made of matter.

B. Color is a property of matter. Use this property to put the objects into groups.
   1. What are the colors of the groups?

C. Think of another property of matter. Use this property to put the objects into new groups.
   2. How are the objects in each group alike?

D. Repeat step **C.** See how many ways you can group the objects.

E. Compare your groups with those of other students.

Conclusion

1. What are some properties of matter?
2. How many properties did you identify?

Using science ideas

Make a collection of objects such as rocks, leaves, or stamps. Use their properties to group the objects.

STATES OF MATTER

What are the states of matter?

Have you ever blown up a balloon? If you have, you know that you filled the balloon with air. The air takes up space and it has mass. The air inside the balloon is made of matter.

Matter can be found in different forms. Matter may be a solid or a liquid (lik'wid). Or, like the air inside the balloon, matter may be a gas. The states of matter are **solid, liquid,** and **gas.**

You can see all three states of matter in this picture of a fish tank. The glass tank is solid matter. The water inside the tank is liquid matter. And the air bubbles are gas.

Filling a balloon

A solid, a liquid, and a gas

Now look around. Name things you see that are solid, liquid, or gas. You may see many solids and liquids. But most times you cannot see gas.

Each state of matter has different properties. Solids have a shape of their own. The shape of most solids does not change. But solids are found in many different shapes. Look at the rocks this boy has collected. Rocks are solid. Look at the different shapes of the rocks.

Looking at a rock collection

Liquids are not like solids. Liquids never have a shape of their own. They always have the same shape as their container. This means that the same liquid in different containers will have different shapes. In the picture you can see milk in the glass and in the straw. The milk changes shape as it is moved from the glass up through the straw. When all the milk is gone, what do you think will fill the glass and the straw? Both will be filled with another kind of matter, a gas.

Liquid changing shape

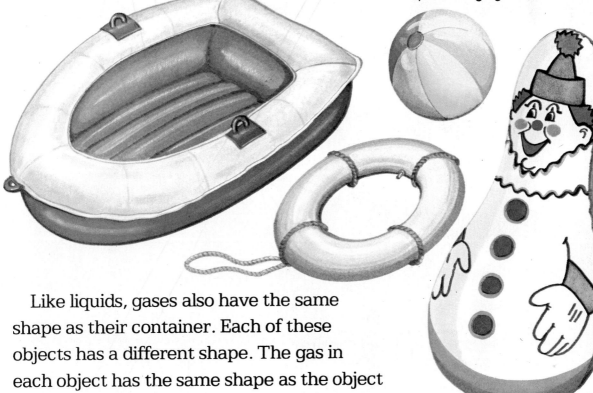

Like liquids, gases also have the same shape as their container. Each of these objects has a different shape. The gas in each object has the same shape as the object it fills.

Gas-filled objects

93

THE PARTICLES IN MATTER
What is matter made of?

Why are solids, liquids, and gases so different from each other? To answer this, you must learn more about matter. All matter is made of small particles (pär'tə kəlz) called **atoms** (at'əmz). There are many kinds of atoms. They are so small that you cannot see them. Atoms join together in different ways to form larger particles of matter. Many of these particles join to form the matter around you.

In the drawings you can see how close particles are in different states of matter. In the solid they are close together. In the liquid they are farther apart. And in the gas they are even farther apart.

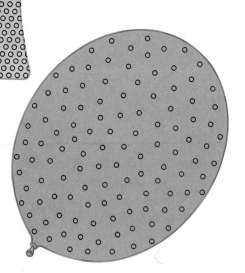

The particles in matter are always moving. But you cannot see them or feel them move. Look at the drawings. The arrows show how much the particles in matter move. In solids, the close particles move back and forth, or vibrate. But they never change places. This is why most solids do not change shape. The particles in liquids move more than those in solids. They roll over each other. This is why liquids have no shape of their own. The particles in gases move the most. They bump into each other. They spread out to fill any container. The states of matter are different because the particles in them behave differently.

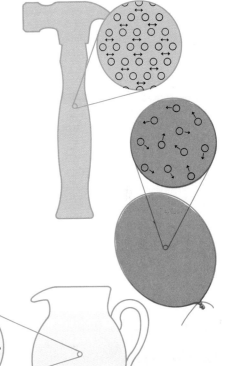

How can you show that the particles in a liquid are always moving? Fill a glass jar with water. Put the jar in a place where it will not be moved. Gently put 2 drops of food coloring into the water. Watch what happens to the water. Look at the water again in a few minutes. Let the jar stand overnight. Look at the water the next day. Try to explain why the color spread through the water.

MATTER CAN CHANGE
How does matter change?

Matter can change from one state to another. This kind of change is called a **physical** (fiz′ə kəl) **change.** Changes in size and shape are also physical changes. In a physical change, you have the same kind of matter before and after the change.

Water is matter. When water is poured, it is a liquid. If the water is put into a freezer, it changes to ice. If the water is heated enough, it will form a gas. Water in the form of a gas is called **water vapor** (vā′pər).

Changing size and shape

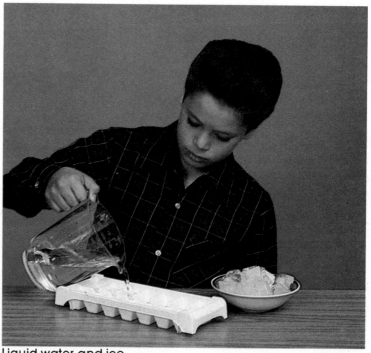
Liquid water and ice

These changes in water show that matter can change from a liquid to a solid. It also shows that a liquid can change to a gas. Water may change from one state to another. But it is always water. It never changes to anything else.

Ice starts to form when water is cooled to zero degrees Celsius (sel'sē əs). (The symbol for degrees Celsius is °C.) This temperature (tem'pər ə chər) is the **freezing point** of water. At 0°C, the moving particles in water slow down to form ice. The water in this pond is frozen. How will the ice change on a warm day?

Frozen pond

Icicle melting

Water begins to boil at 100°C. This is the **boiling point** of water. As water boils, its particles move faster and farther apart. The particles then escape to form steam.

Water evaporating

Water condensing

In the picture, steam is rising from boiling water. But water does not have to boil to change to a gas. Moving particles of water are always escaping from the surface to form water vapor. This change from a liquid to a gas is called **evaporation** (i vap ə-rā'shen).

Water vapor can change back to a liquid. This kind of change is called **condensation** (kon den sā'shən). Condensation takes place when water vapor is cooled. If you breathe on a cool window, water vapor from your breath changes into liquid water.

Do you know?

A thermometer (thər mom'ə-tər) is used to measure temperature. The liquid inside a thermometer rises when it is warm. And when it is cool, the liquid falls. Why does the liquid rise and fall as the temperature changes? Warm liquid takes up more space than cool liquid. As the liquid becomes warmer, its particles move farther apart and the liquid takes up more space.

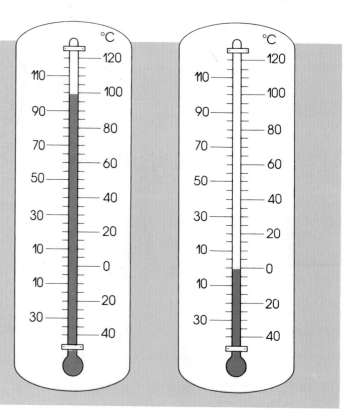

—DIFFERENT KINDS OF MATTER—

How can one kind of matter become different matter?

You learned that matter, such as water, may change from one state to another. This is a physical change. Matter may change in another way.

Firewood

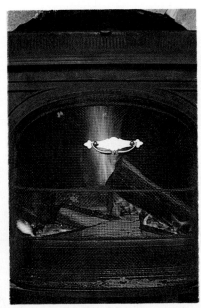
Burning wood

Ashes

Some matter can become different matter. This kind of change is called a **chemical** (kem′ə kəl) **change.** Burning causes wood to change to ashes. In the pictures you can see that wood and ashes do not look the same. Is there any way to change the ashes back to wood?

How can different matter form?

Materials bottle / baking soda / 2 funnels / spoon / balloon / vinegar

Procedure
A. Put 1 spoonful of baking soda into a bottle. Use a funnel.

B. Use a different funnel to pour some vinegar into a balloon.

C. Put the open end of the balloon over the top of the bottle.

D. Lift the other end of the balloon so that the vinegar goes into the bottle.
   1. What do you see happening?

E. When the vinegar and baking soda mix, there is a chemical change. Different matter is formed. This matter is a gas called carbon dioxide.
   2. How is the carbon dioxide different from the baking soda?
   3. How is the carbon dioxide different from the vinegar?

Conclusion
1. What caused carbon dioxide to form?
2. What did the carbon dioxide look like?

Using science ideas
Baking soda is sometimes used in cakes. What would happen if the baking soda was left out of a cake?

Sometimes different matter is formed when two or more kinds of matter are mixed together. These children are making bread. To do this, they are mixing many special things together. The bread will not be like the things it is made from. The bread will be different matter.

Mixing different kinds of matter

New matter

IDEAS TO REMEMBER

► Matter is anything that takes up space and has mass.
► The states of matter are solid, liquid, and gas.
► All matter is made of atoms.
► Some kinds of matter can change from one state to another.
► Some kinds of matter can become different matter.

Reviewing the Chapter

SCIENCE WORDS

A. Copy the sentences below. Use science terms from the chapter to complete the sentences.

1. The three states of matter are ____, ____, and ____.
2. The temperature 0°C is the ____ point of water.
3. New matter is formed in a ____ change.
4. Water in the form of a gas is called water ____.
5. The measure of how much matter there is in an object is called ____.
6. The temperature 100°C is the ____ point of water.
7. Melting is an example of a ____ change.

B. Write the letter of the term that best matches the definition. Not all the terms will be used.

1. Smallest particle of matter
2. The change from a gas to a liquid
3. Tool to measure mass
4. Matter that takes the shape of its container
5. The change from a liquid to a gas
6. Matter that has a shape of its own

    a. evaporation
    b. solid
    c. mass
    d. condensation
    e. atom
    f. liquid
    g. balance

UNDERSTANDING IDEAS

A. Make a chart like the one shown. Write the names of 10 objects from the chapter under the correct headings.

Solid	Liquid	Gas

B. Copy the list below. Next to each item write *P* if it describes a physical change. Write *C* if it describes a chemical change.

1. sawing wood   **5.** breaking glass

2. chopping onions   **6.** melting butter

3. slicing bread   **7.** baking bread

4. burning wood   **8.** cutting paper

C. Write a recipe that uses two or more kinds of matter to make different matter. What is needed to make the matter change?

USING IDEAS

1. Find out if all liquids have the same freezing point. Label two paper cups *A* and *B*. Half fill both cups with water. Put a teaspoon of salt into cup *A* and stir. Put both cups into the freezer. Check the cups every half hour. Which cup of water starts to freeze first?

Chapter 6

Force, Work, and Energy

These people are putting up a new building. To do this job, they must move ground, cement, and steel. You can see that a lot of pushing, pulling, and lifting is needed. Some is being done by people and some is being done by machines. What things are being pushed or pulled? What things are being lifted?

In this chapter you will learn more about pushing, pulling, and lifting. You will also learn about the energy needed to do these things.

FORCES
What do forces do?

Look at the pictures. Sometimes you push to make things move, and sometimes you pull. You push or pull even when you lift something. A push or a pull is a **force** (fôrs). Force is always needed to make something move.

Pushing   Pulling

It takes more force to move some things than it does to move others. For example, suppose that you lifted a big dictionary. Then you lifted a smaller book. You would use a different amount of force to lift each one. Which would take more force to lift, the dictionary or the smaller book?

This boy is using a pulling force. He is using force not to make the dog move but to make it stop. Force must be used to make things slow down or stop moving.

In this picture the skier is using a pushing force on her pole to turn. Force must also be used to make moving things change their direction.

In all of these examples, forces change the motion of things. When something that is standing still starts to move, its motion changes. Stopping is a change in motion. Speeding up, slowing down, and turning are all changes in motion. Pushing or pulling forces are needed to cause all of these changes.

KINDS OF FORCES

What are some pushing and pulling forces?

Why is this diver falling toward the water? You cannot see anything pushing or pulling her. What is making her move? The force that is making the diver move is gravity (grav'ə tē). **Gravity** is the force of one object pulling on another object. The earth pulls on all things with this force. Rain, snow, and leaves always fall to the ground. A ball thrown into the air always falls to the ground. The earth's gravity pulls all these things toward the ground.

Measuring the pull of gravity

The earth's gravity pulls on some things more than on others. Objects with more mass are pulled more by the earth's gravity. For example, a bowling ball is pulled toward the earth more than a basketball is. The bowling ball has more mass.

When you weigh something, you are measuring the pull of the earth's gravity. Suppose you weigh 31 kilograms and a friend weighs 27 kilograms. Who is pulled more by gravity?

How can you measure force?

Materials tape / rubber band / metric ruler / paper clip / several small objects

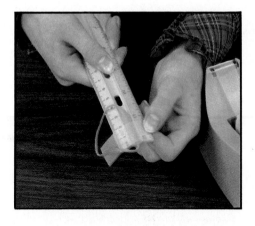

Procedure

A. Tape one end of a rubber band to a metric ruler as shown. The end of the rubber band should be even with the end of the ruler.

B. Open a paper clip to make a hook. Hang the paper clip from the free end of the rubber band.
   1. At what mark on the ruler is the free end of the rubber band?

C. Make a chart like the one shown. Fill in the chart as you do steps **D** to **F.**

D. Hold the ruler as shown. Hang a small object on the hook.
   2. How many centimeters did the rubber band stretch?

E. Place the object on your desk. Then pull it by moving the ruler.
   3. How many centimeters did the rubber band stretch?

F. Lift and pull some other small objects.
   4. How many centimeters did the rubber band stretch when lifting each object?
   5. How many centimeters did the rubber band stretch when pulling each object?

Object	Centimeters (lifting)	Centimeters (pulling)

Conclusion

1. Why did some objects stretch the rubber band more than others?

2. Is more force needed to lift an object or to pull it?

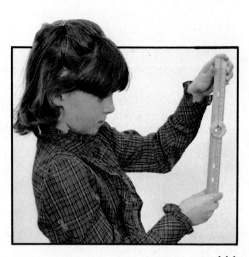

This picture shows another kind of force at work. The motion of the paper clips changed when they were lifted. Magnetism (mag′nə tiz əm) caused this change. **Magnetism** is a force that acts on some kinds of metal.

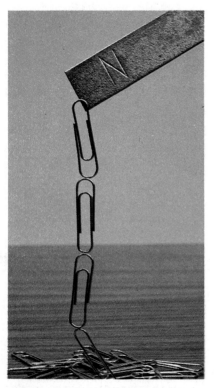

Magnet lifting paper clips

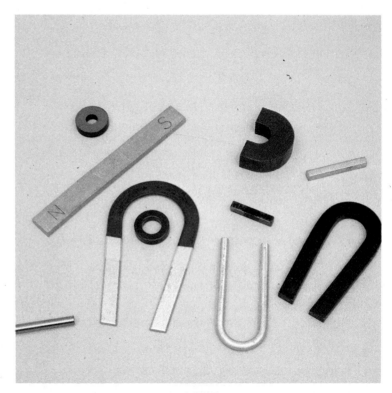

Different shapes and kinds of magnets

If you have ever used magnets, you know that magnetism is not like gravity. Gravity is only a pulling force. But magnetism sometimes pulls and sometimes pushes.

Magnets have two ends. They are called the north pole and the south pole. There is a pulling force between a north pole and a south pole. Two north poles or two south poles push each other away.

Have you ever played shuffleboard? After you push the disk, it slides across the floor. As it moves, it slows down until it stops. Slowing down and stopping are changes in the motion of the disk.

The force that causes this change in motion is friction (frik'shən). **Friction** is a force that slows down or stops motion. It is produced by one thing rubbing against another. If there were no friction, the shuffleboard disk would keep on moving.

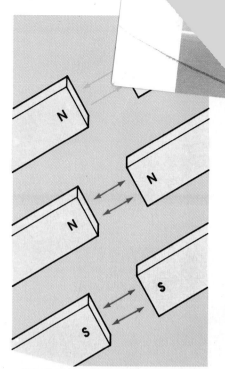

PULLING AND PUSHING FORCES
BETWEEN THE POLES OF MAGNETS

Oiling a hinge

What happens when you rub your hands together? Do your hands feel warmer? Friction produces heat. Objects that rub always become warmer. What would happen if you made your hands slippery with soap and water? There would be less friction then. Your hands would not feel as warm. Anything that reduces friction is called a **lubricant** (lü'brə kənt). Oil is one kind of lubricant. Grease is another kind of lubricant. What other lubricants can you name?

Finding out

How is friction increased or reduced? Make a slide from a piece of heavy smooth cardboard. Use books to prop up one end. Let a smooth flat stone go down the slide. Notice how fast it moves.

Lay the cardboard flat and rub one side with sandpaper to make it rough. Set up the slide again. Find out if the stone slides faster or slower on the rough cardboard.

Turn the cardboard over and lay it flat. Rub a bar of soap all over this side. Set up the slide again. Find out if the stone slides faster or slower than before.

When did the slide have the least friction? The most friction?

WORK
When do you do work?

Look at the picture. Where is work being done? **Work** is done when a force is used to move something. For example, you do work if you push a chair across a room. Suppose someone sat on the chair. Then you would have to push harder to move it. You would be using more force, so you would be doing more work.

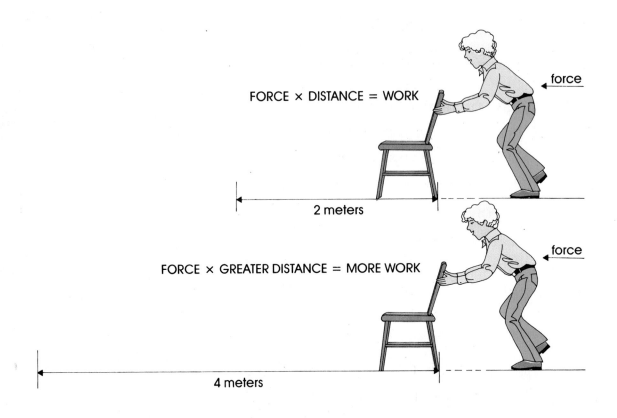

FORCE × DISTANCE = WORK

force

2 meters

FORCE × GREATER DISTANCE = MORE WORK

force

4 meters

You also do more work if you move something a greater distance. Suppose that you move a chair 2 meters. The next time, you move it 4 meters. Four meters is a greater distance than 2 meters. When you move the chair 4 meters, you do more work.

The amount of work that is done always depends on two things. It depends on how much force is used to move an object. And it depends on how far the object moves. Look at the picture. Is the person pushing against the wall doing work? Why or why not?

ENERGY
How is energy used to do work?

Do you feel tired after you do work? You may feel that way because you have used up energy. **Energy** is the ability to do work. Energy is used whenever a force moves something.

There are many different kinds of energy. One kind is heat energy. In the picture heat energy is being used to make the balloon rise. So heat energy is being used to do work.

Electricity (i lek tris'ə tē) is another kind of energy. It is used to run a motor attached to the garage door. This motor puts a force on the door. The force moves the door upward. Work is done as the door moves.

Hot-air balloon

Electric garage-door opener

117

How can water do work?

Materials milk carton, 2-liter / scissors / round pencil / tape / piece of string, about 45 centimeters long / paper clip / plastic pitcher / water

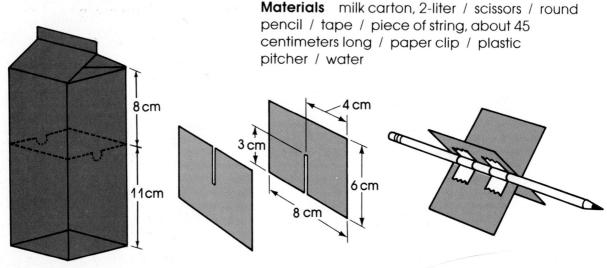

Procedure

A. Cut a milk carton as shown by the dotted line. From the top part, cut two pieces of cardboard, 8 centimeters × 6 centimeters. Cut slits in the pieces of cardboard. Fit the pieces together at the slits. Tape a pencil to the cardboard as shown. You have made a waterwheel.

B. Tie one end of a piece of string to a paper clip. Tie the other end of the string to the end of the pencil.

C. Cut notches in two sides of the bottom part of the carton as shown. Place the carton at the edge of a table. Lay the pencil in the notches. The paper clip should hang down over the edge of the table.

   1. Describe what will happen if water is poured on the waterwheel.

D. Slowly pour water onto the waterwheel.

   2. Describe what happens.

   3. Was work done?

Conclusion

How do you know water did work?

Some other kinds of energy are light, sound, and motion energy. Motion energy is the energy of moving things. An elevator has motion energy as it moves up and down. Water also has motion energy that can be used to do work. Look around you. Where do you see other examples of motion energy? You have motion energy also. You have it when you run, write with a pencil, or move in any way.

Outdoor elevators

IDEAS TO REMEMBER

- ▶ A force is a push or a pull.
- ▶ Forces can change the motion of things.
- ▶ Gravity, magnetism, and friction are forces.
- ▶ Work is done when a force moves something.
- ▶ Energy is used to do work.
- ▶ Light, heat, electricity, sound, and motion energy are kinds of energy.

Waterwheel

Reviewing the Chapter

SCIENCE WORDS

A. Copy the sentences below. Use science terms from the chapter to complete the sentences.

1. The force that pulls things toward the earth is ___ .

2. A material, such as oil, that reduces friction is called a ___ .

3. A force that may be a push or a pull and that acts on certain metals is ___ .

4. When a force is used to move something, ___ is done.

5. The force that slows down or stops the motion of objects that rub against one another is ___ .

B. Identify each of the following.

1. I am used whenever a force moves something. I am the ability to do work. What am I?

2. I must be used to make moving things change their direction. I may be a push or a pull. What am I?

UNDERSTANDING IDEAS

A. Name three kinds of energy. Give an example of each.

B. The drawings show different things happening. For each drawing, name the force that is causing something to happen.

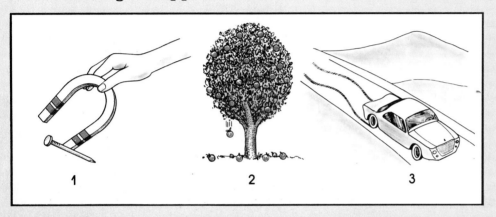

C. Who did more work? Explain your answer.

1. Lisa carried a bowling ball. Jane carried a tennis ball.
2. Tom moved the desk 1 meter. Juan moved it 3 meters.

USING IDEAS

1. Make a bulletin board display showing objects being pushed or pulled by different forces.
2. On the moon, the pull of gravity is about one sixth of what it is on the earth. Divide your weight by 6 to find out what you would weigh on the moon.

Chapter 7

Machines

This girl is using a hammer to drive a nail into a piece of wood. She could not do this work using only her hands. So she is using a hammer. A hammer is a tool.

People use many other tools to help them with their work. All these tools are kinds of machines. Name some of the other machines in the picture. How can each be used to make work easier?

In this chapter you will learn about many different kinds of machines. You will also learn how machines help people with their work.

- THE LEVER—A SIMPLE MACHINE -
How does a lever help do work?

People do many kinds of work each day. Sometimes they use machines when they work. A **machine** is something that helps people do work. Not all machines are the same. Some machines, like cars, have many moving parts. Other machines have few or no moving parts. They are called **simple machines.** A snow shovel is a simple machine. How is it different from a snowplow?

Machines

Using a snow shovel

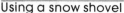

Using a snowplow

Using a lever

A **lever** (lev′ər) is a simple machine. Levers are often used to lift or move things. These children are using a lever to move a heavy rock. To do this work, they must use force to push down on the tree branch. The object that will be moved, the rock, is called the **load.** The force and the load move in opposite directions.

As the lever moves the rock, it moves on a turning point. The turning point here is the log. Levers always use a force, a load, and a turning point when work is done.

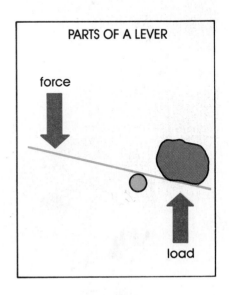

PARTS OF A LEVER

force

load

125

Riding a seesaw

Opening a jar

Pulling a nail

Have you ever ridden on a seesaw? If you have, then you have used a lever to lift someone. And that person used the same lever to lift you. Look at the first picture of the seesaw. Find the force, the load, and the turning point. Now look at the second picture. Did the force and the load change? How can you tell?

Not all levers look the same. Some are much shorter than a seesaw. This is a short lever. It is being used to open a jar. It would be hard to open the jar without using a lever like this.

This hammer is being used as a lever. It is being used to pull a nail out of wood. Where is the force coming from? What is the load? Do you think it would be easy to pull a nail without using a lever?

How does a lever work?

Materials 3 pencils / tape / wooden ruler / 2 small paper cups / small rock / paper clips

Procedure

A. Tape three pencils together.

B. Tape a small paper cup to each end of a wooden ruler.

C. Balance the ruler on the pencils.

D. Put a small rock into one of the cups.

E. Put paper clips, one at a time, into the other cup until the rock is lifted.
  1. How many paper clips were needed?

F. Empty both cups. Move one of the cups so that it is closer to the center of the ruler. Tape it. Put the small rock into this cup. Repeat step **E.**
  2. How many paper clips were needed to lift the rock?

Conclusion

1. What part of the lever is the turning point? What part is the load? What part is the force?
2. When the load is moved closer to the turning point, what happens to the amount of force needed?

Using science ideas
How is the lever in this activity like the seesaw in the pictures on page 126?

— USING AN INCLINED PLANE —
How is an inclined plane used?

These people are using a ramp. A ramp makes it easier for them to put their things into the truck. A ramp is higher at one end than at the other. It is called an **inclined** (in klīnd′) **plane.** An inclined plane is a simple machine. It can help in moving an object to a higher place.

Any slanted surface can be an inclined plane. A slanted board and a path going up a hill are both inclined planes. Some inclined

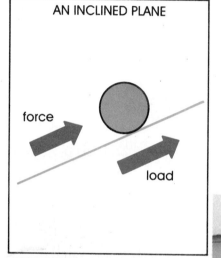

AN INCLINED PLANE

force

load

Using a ramp

Different kinds of ramps

planes are very steep. Others are not. It takes more force to move up a steep inclined plane. In all inclined planes the force and the load move in the same direction.

Inclined planes are used in many places. Some are ramps for cars and trucks to use. Others are ramps for people to use. Maybe some of your toys have ramps. Think of other places where you have seen inclined planes.

Two inclined planes together make a simple machine called a **wedge** (wej). They come together to form a V-shaped edge. A wedge can be used to cut and split things apart. An ax is a wedge. Would you be able to split wood with the other side of an ax?

Ax and log

129

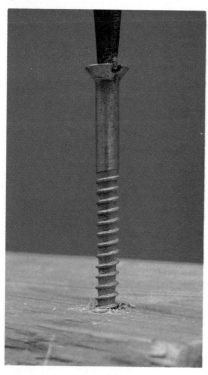

Turning a screw

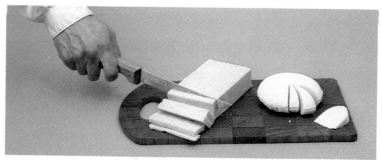

Care should always be used with cutting tools.

Many other cutting tools are wedges. Nails and pins are also wedges. But they are very small. Can you name other wedges?

A **screw** is like an inclined plane that is wrapped around a center post. A screw must be turned to move into wood. Many jars have screw lids.

Finding out

Can you show that a screw is like an inclined plane that is wrapped around a post? Use a sheet of paper that measures about 12 centimeters by 24 centimeters. Draw a line from the upper left-hand corner to the lower right-hand corner. Use a ruler and a crayon. The line must be thick and straight. Now cut the paper along the line you have drawn. Does your paper look like an inclined plane? Place the paper triangle with the line on your desk. Lay it so that the line faces down. Line up your pencil with the shortest side of the triangle. Roll the paper tightly around the pencil. Now, do you know how a screw is like an inclined plane?

How does an inclined plane make work easier?

Materials   scale to measure force / small object / 6 books / board

Procedure

A. Make a chart like the one shown. Write the answers to the questions below on your chart.

B. Lift a small object using a scale to measure force.
   1. How far does the rubber band stretch?

C. Place two books under one end of a board to make a ramp. Use the scale to pull the object up the ramp.
   2. How far does the rubber band stretch?

D. Place two more books under the board. Use the scale to pull the object up the ramp.
   3. How far does the rubber band stretch?

E. Place two more books under the board. This will make the ramp very steep. Use the scale to pull the object up the ramp.
   4. How far does the rubber band stretch?

Conclusion

1. When was the most force needed to move the object?
2. When was the least force needed to move the object?

Using science ideas
It is hard for people to walk up ramps that are very steep. Explain why.

Moving the object	Centimeters of stretch
Lifting	
Using 2 books	
Using 4 books	
Using 6 books	

THE WHEEL AND AXLE
How does a wheel and axle make work easier?

There are many doors in your school and at home. You use a doorknob to open most of these doors. A doorknob is a simple machine called a wheel and axle (ak'səl). A **wheel and axle** is made of a wheel that turns on a center post. The center post is the axle. The wheel and axle makes it easier to turn and move things. Find the wheel and axle on the doorknob.

Turning a doorknob

Wheel-and-axle objects

There are many other examples of a wheel and axle. Sometimes a wheel and axle is easy to recognize. It is found on a bicycle, a wagon, and roller skates. All these things move on wheels. Name some other things that move on wheels.

Sometimes a wheel and axle is not so easy to recognize. Think of the steering wheel of a car. Here the axle is the steering column. A steering wheel allows a driver to turn the car. A driver does not have to use much force to do this. Less force is needed when the steering wheel is large. This is why many trucks have larger steering wheels than cars do. It would be hard for truck drivers to turn corners without large steering wheels.

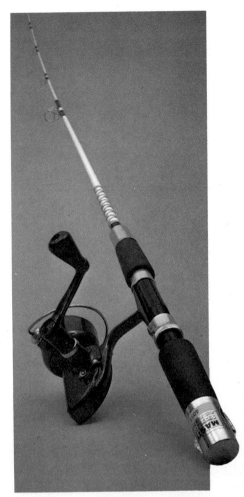
Fishing rod and reel

Steering wheel and column

Turning a corner

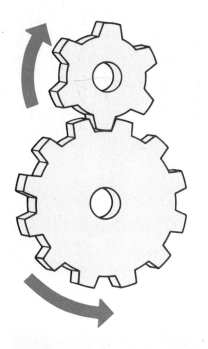

A gear is a special kind of wheel and axle. A **gear** is a wheel with teeth. The teeth allow one gear to turn another. In the picture the large gear has more teeth than the smaller gear. The teeth of this large gear fit the teeth of the smaller gear. When the large gear turns, the smaller one does, too.

Gears are used in watches, cars, and many other machines. Here you can see the gears in an eggbeater. The beaters at the bottom turn faster than the handle. The gears in an eggbeater make it easier to mix things.

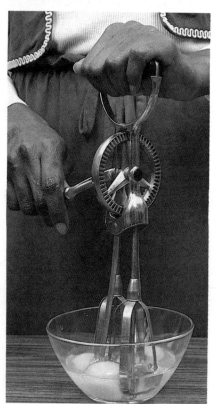

Using an eggbeater

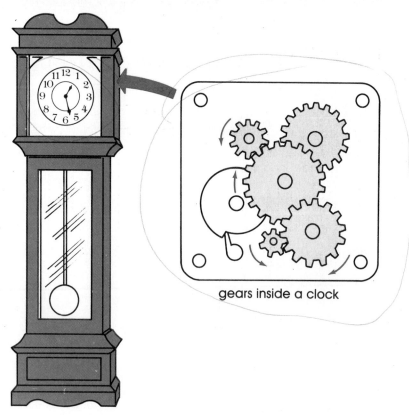

gears inside a clock

PULLEYS
When are pulleys used?

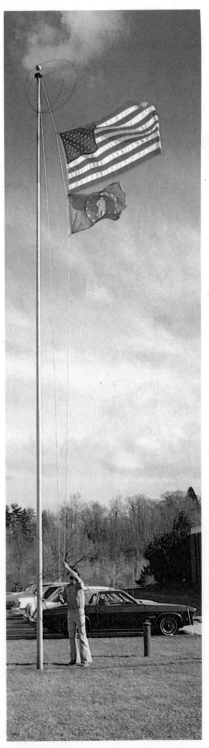

This man is raising flags on a pole. He could not do this job without using a simple machine called a pulley (pül'ē). A **pulley** is a wheel with a rope around it. The rope fits into a groove on the wheel. As the man pulls down on the rope, the flags are raised higher. The force and the load move in opposite directions.

Pulleys are used to move objects up, down, or sideways. They are also used to move objects, such as flags, to places that are hard to reach.

A FIXED PULLEY

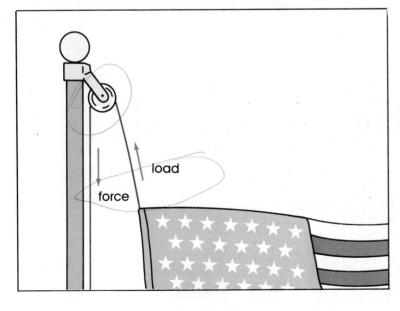

load

force

Raising flags

Moving drapes

The pulley on the flagpole is called a fixed pulley. A **fixed pulley** stays in one place. Fixed pulleys are used to move some kinds of shades and drapes. Find the pulley that will be used to move the drapes.

Some pulleys are used to lift heavy loads. These pulleys move as the load is moved. They are called **movable pulleys.**

Usually a movable pulley is used together with a fixed pulley. The load is attached to the movable pulley. A single rope passes between both pulleys. When the rope is pulled, the load is raised. It is easy to move a heavy load in this way. Find a fixed pulley and a movable pulley in the picture.

Lifting a heavy load

COMPOUND MACHINES
What are compound machines?

Many of the machines that people use are compound (kom'pound) machines. **Compound machines** are made of two or more simple machines. Scissors (siz'ərz) are made of two levers that work together. The cutting edges of scissors are shaped like wedges.

Sharpening a pencil

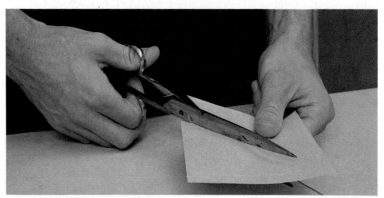

Cutting paper

Look at this pencil sharpener. The cover has been taken off. Which simple machines can you see? The handle is a wheel that turns on an axle. Another part of the sharpener looks like a screw. A compound machine like this one makes it fast and easy for you to sharpen a pencil. You probably use many other compound machines in school and at home.

IDEAS TO REMEMBER

▶ Machines help people to do work.
▶ Simple machines have few or no moving parts.
▶ The lever, inclined plane, wheel and axle, and pulley are simple machines.
▶ Compound machines are made of two or more simple machines.

Reviewing the Chapter

SCIENCE WORDS

A. Copy the sentences below. Use science terms from the chapter to complete the sentences.

1. Machines having few or no moving parts are called ___.
2. A ramp, which is higher at one end than at the other, is called an ___.
3. A wheel with teeth is called a ___.
4. Two inclined planes together make a ___.
5. A ___ is a wheel with a rope around it.
6. A ___ is like an inclined plane that is wrapped around a center post.
7. A ___ is made of a wheel that turns on a center post.
8. A ___ always moves on a turning point.

B. Unscramble each group of letters to find a science term from the chapter. Write a sentence using each term.

1. munpodoc namiche
2. xedif lepluy
3. odal
4. emobavl lepluy
5. lepmis henicam
6. rocef

UNDERSTANDING IDEAS

A. Name each of the simple machines pictured below. Explain how each helps to make work easier.

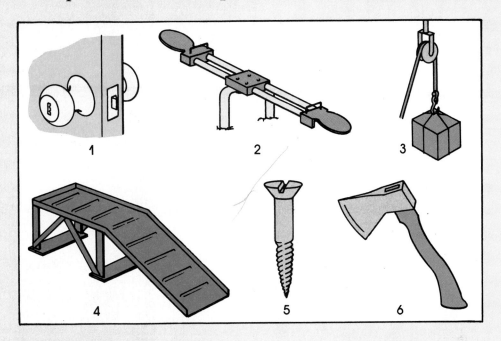

1
2
3
4
5
6

B. Compare a fixed pulley with a movable pulley. List some uses of each.

USING IDEAS

1. Invent a compound machine made of at least three simple machines. Draw a picture of your invention. Label the simple machines in the drawing.

2. List machines found in the classroom, on the playground, and at home. Make a bar graph showing the number of machines found in each of these places.

Chapter 8

Sound

Sounds are all around you. A busy street in the middle of a city has many kinds of sounds. Imagine you are standing on the sidewalk at this place in the city. What sounds would you hear? How would the sounds be different? What sounds would be unpleasant? What sounds would be useful?

In this chapter you will learn about sound. You will learn how sounds are made and how they are different. You will also learn how sound moves.

MAKING SOUND

How is sound made?

Listen carefully to the sounds around you. Sound is a form of energy. Sound comes from matter that moves back and forth, or vibrates (vī'brāts). The back-and-forth movement is called **vibration** (vī brā'shən). A drum vibrates when it is hit. The ruler in one of the pictures is vibrating. What caused it to vibrate? Each of these objects makes sound when it vibrates.

You have learned that all matter is made of small particles. Sound moves through matter by making the particles vibrate. Without these particles of matter, sound could not move from place to place.

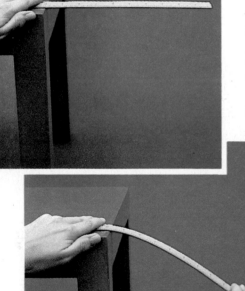

When a guitar string is plucked, it vibrates. The vibrating string makes the air particles around it move back and forth. These vibrating particles cause the particles next to them to vibrate. The vibration is passed from one particle to another. Soon particles far from the string are vibrating. In this way sound moves from place to place.

Sound moves in waves. The sound waves move through the air in every direction. The drawing shows how sound moves away from a ringing bell. People around the bell can hear the sound. It does not make any difference where they stand.

Plucked guitar string vibrating

DIFFERENT SOUNDS

How are sounds different?

You know that sounds are different. There are loud sounds and soft sounds. The loudness or softness of a sound is called **volume** (vol'yəm). A loud sound has more volume than a soft sound. Look at the picture. If the drum is hit softly, the sound will be soft. If it is hit harder, the sound will be louder. The harder the drum is hit, the more it will vibrate. The air around the drum will also vibrate more, so the sound will be louder.

Making a kettledrum vibrate

Another difference in sound is called pitch. **Pitch** is the highness or lowness of sound. Have you ever heard a tuba and a flute? They sound different. The tuba has a low pitch. The flute has a higher pitch.

The speed of vibrations controls the pitch. Fast vibrations make sounds that have a high pitch. Slow vibrations make sounds that have a low pitch. The flute makes air particles vibrate fast. The tuba makes air particles vibrate slowly.

Bands use instruments that make many kinds of sounds. The sounds are not the same even though the volume may be the same.

Playing a tuba

Some of the wind instruments in a band

Playing a flute

How are sounds different?

Materials   shoe box / scissors / 3 rubber bands of different thicknesses

Procedure

A. Remove the lid from a shoe box. Use the scissors to cut a rectangular opening in the lid, as shown in the picture. The opening should be about 15 centimeters long and 5 centimeters wide.

B. Place the lid onto the box. Place three rubber bands around the box. They should stretch over the opening. The rubber bands should be about 3 centimeters apart.
   1. How will the sound be different if you lightly pluck each rubber band?

C. Lightly pluck each rubber band.
   2. How are the sounds different?
   3. Which rubber band has the highest pitch?
   4. Which rubber band has the lowest pitch?

Conclusion
What causes the difference in pitch among the rubber bands?

Using science ideas
1. How could you change this experiment to get different sounds?
2. Why does a violin or a guitar have strings of different thicknesses?

HOW SOUND MOVES

How does sound move through different kinds of matter?

Sound moves through all kinds of matter. You know it moves through air. Sound also moves through liquid and solid matter. In fact, sound moves differently through liquids and solids than through gases such as air.

The particles in gases are farther apart than those in liquids and solids. The distance between particles affects how well the particles can pass vibrations to each other. It is harder to send vibrations through matter when the particles are far apart. Since particles in air are farther apart, air does not carry vibrations as well as a liquid.

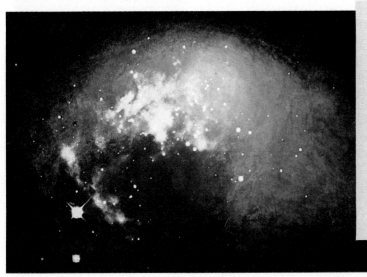

Do you know?

There is no sound in outer space. You could not hear a gunshot from a meter away. There is no air in outer space. Particles are not present to pass vibrations to each other. Without vibrating particles sound cannot reach your ears.

SPEED OF SOUND	
Type of matter	Speed (in meters per second)
Air	340
Water	1500
Wood	3500
Rock	3700

Sound also moves through different matter at different speeds. Sound moves fastest through solids. It moves slowest through gases like air.

Look at the table. It shows the speed of sound through different kinds of matter. In what unit is speed measured? What is the speed of sound in air? What is the speed of sound in water? Why is the speed of sound through wood nearly the same as it is through rock?

Finding out

Can you use sound to measure distance? Light travels at a much faster speed than sound does. When lightning strikes, you see it instantly. Sound moves at a much slower speed. So you hear thunder after you see lightning. The more time there is between seeing lightning and hearing thunder, the more distance there is between you and the lightning.

You can measure the distance of lightning. Count how many seconds there are between lightning and thunder. Sound takes 3 seconds to move 1 kilometer. When you see lightning, count how many seconds it takes before you hear thunder. Divide the number of seconds by 3. The answer will be the distance of the lightning in kilometers. How far away is lightning if it takes 12 seconds before you hear the thunder?

How does sound move through matter?

Materials   windup clock / metric ruler / self-sealing plastic bag

Procedure

A. Place a windup clock on a table. Use a metric ruler to measure a distance of 100 centimeters from the clock. Listen to the clock from that distance.

    1. Can you hear the clock through the air?

B. Measure 100 centimeters from the clock on the table. Place your ear on the table at this point. Listen to the clock.

    2. Can you hear the clock through the table?

    3. If you can hear the clock, how does it sound?

C. Fill a self-sealing plastic bag with water. Seal the bag and hold it against your ear. Have a classmate hold the clock against the bag of water.

    4. Can you hear the clock through the bag of water?

    5. If you can hear the clock, how does it sound?

Conclusion

Does sound move best through a solid, a liquid, or a gas?

Using science ideas

Does sound move differently through some solids than it does through others? How could you find out?

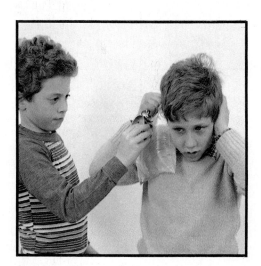

── HOW SOUND BOUNCES ──
What happens when sounds strike different objects?

Sound moves all around us. It bounces off many surfaces. These sounds are reflected sounds. A **reflected sound** is one whose direction of movement has changed. A ball that is thrown against a wall bounces in another direction. Sounds that strike objects reflect, or bounce, in other directions, too.

The drawing shows how sound reflects from different surfaces. The sound that strikes a smooth surface reflects in one direction. The direction in which the sound reflects depends on how it strikes the surface. In what direction does sound reflect from a rough surface?

How sound is reflected

Have you ever heard an echo (ek'ō)? An **echo** is a reflected sound. Echoes can be heard best in places where a hard surface is facing the source of sound.

Some surfaces absorb sound. They absorb sound like a sponge absorbs water. Sounds that are absorbed cannot bounce around.

Unfurnished room

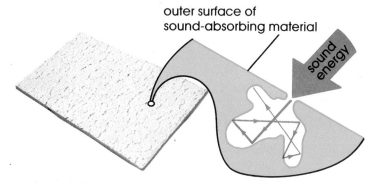

outer surface of sound-absorbing material

sound energy

Sound-absorbing material

Furnished room

Drapes absorb sound. Carpets and soft furniture also absorb sound. In which of these rooms would sound be absorbed better?

Finding out

What is the best sound absorber? Place a ticking alarm clock in a box. Make a small hole in the box. Place your ear near the hole. Listen to the sound of the ticking clock. Now use different materials to put around the clock. You can use wood, cloth, paper, and sponges. What other materials can you use? With each different material listen to the clock. Which one best absorbs the sound?

SOUNDS MADE BY LIVING THINGS

How do living things make sounds?

Sounds can be very interesting. Some of the most interesting sounds are made by animals. Animals and people use sounds to send messages to each other. The sending of these messages is called **communication** (kə myü nə kā′shən).

You communicate by sound when you talk. You talk by using the vocal (vō′kəl) cords in your throat. **Vocal cords** are special flaps of muscle that vibrate when you talk. The different vibrations of your vocal cords make different sounds. Your mouth and tongue help form these sounds.

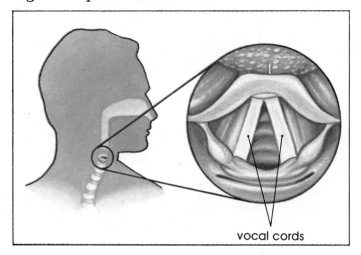

vocal cords

Animals make sounds in many ways. Have you ever heard frogs and crickets at night? They make sounds in strange ways.

The spring peeper is a small frog with a big voice. You may have heard spring peepers singing at night. This frog fills a sac in its throat with air. The sac looks like a balloon. The frog uses the air in the sac to increase the volume of the sound it makes.

Crickets do not have vocal cords. They make sound by rapidly rubbing their wings together. This makes the air around them vibrate.

Cricket

Spring peeper

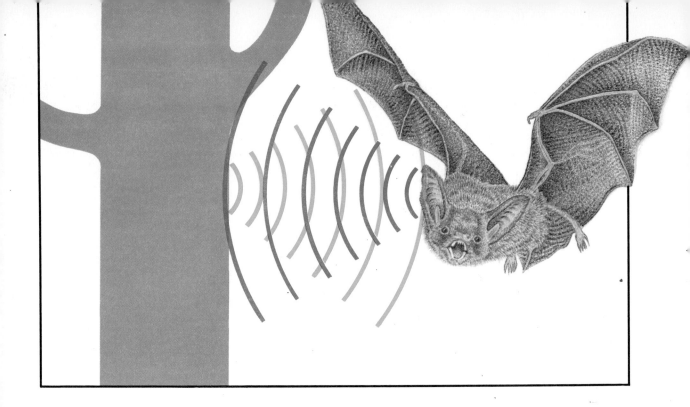

Some animals use sounds to locate objects. They produce sounds with a very high pitch. These sounds cannot be heard by people. Bats are animals that make such sounds. They give off sounds as they fly. These sounds reflect off objects, and the bat hears them echo. The bat uses the echo to find objects. Since bats do not see well, they use sound to find their way around when they fly. Dolphins also find objects by using sound in this way.

Sound is important to people as well as animals. But some people are deaf and cannot hear sound. They communicate with others by using special hand signals.

Dolphins

Teacher using hand signals to communicate with deaf children

IDEAS TO REMEMBER

▶ Sound is a form of energy.
▶ Sound is produced when matter vibrates.
▶ Sound moves in waves in all directions from its source.
▶ The loudness or softness of a sound is called volume.
▶ Pitch is the highness or lowness of a sound.
▶ The speed of sound is fastest in solids and slowest in gases.
▶ An echo is a reflected sound.

Reviewing the Chapter

SCIENCE WORDS

A. Use all the terms below to complete the sentences.

pitch   vibration   reflected sound
volume   matter

Sound comes from __1__ that moves back and forth. This back-and-forth movement is called __2__. Sound moves in waves in all directions. A __3__ is a sound that has changed the direction of its movement. The loudness or softness of a sound is called __4__. The highness or lowness of a sound is called __5__.

B. Write the letter of the term that best matches the definition. Not all the terms will be used.

1. The sending of messages from one to another
2. Produced when matter vibrates
3. Flaps of muscle that vibrate
4. Reflected sound
5. Highness or lowness of sound

   a. vocal cords
   b. echo
   c. sound
   d. volume
   e. pitch
   f. communication

UNDERSTANDING IDEAS

A. Write *T* for the sentences that are true and *F* for the sentences that are false.

1. Sound moves in waves in one direction from its source.
2. Sound is a form of energy.
3. The loudness or softness of sound is called pitch.
4. Slow vibrations make sounds that have a low pitch.
5. Rough surfaces reflect sound better than smooth surfaces.

B. Look at the drawing of a harp. Which strings would you pluck to get a high pitch? Explain your answer.

USING IDEAS

1. Make a list of all the sounds you can hear in your classroom. Next to each sound, write a description of it. Tell if the sound is pleasant or unpleasant, high or low, loud or soft. Discuss your list with other members of the class. Repeat this activity outdoors.

Mechanic

and repair car engines.

Homemakers work with many kinds of machines. Machines make the homemaker's work easier. Some of the machines are simple, but most are compound.

Machines are important to everyone. People use machines in almost everything they do. *Mechanics* (mə kan'iks) tune

Disc jockey

Sound is also used in many ways. *Salespeople* tell about the things they sell. *Radio* and *TV reporters* talk about the news and the weather. A *disc jockey* uses recorded sound when playing records or tapes.

Homemaker

People in Science

Thomas Edison (1847–1931)

Thomas Edison was probably the world's greatest inventor. He is credited with more than 1,000 inventions. His inventions changed the lives of millions of people. Edison was interested in everything. But his greatest invention was the electric light bulb. He also invented the phonograph and a motion-picture machine, among other things.

Edison's phonograph

Developing Skills

WORD SKILLS

Many science words can be broken down into word parts.

Word part	Meaning
mega-	large
son-, sono-	sound
super-	above, over
tele-	far

The tables list some word parts and their meanings.

Word part	Meaning
-gram	drawing
-graph	written
-ic	having to do with
-phone	sound

Use the tables to find the meaning of some science words. You can do this by finding the meaning of each part of the word. For example, the word *telephone* is made of these parts: *tele + phone.*

1. telephone
2. telegraph
3. sonogram
4. megaphone
5. supersonic
6. graphic

READING A TABLE

A table is a list of facts. Different kinds of sounds are listed in the table on the next page. The number next to each kind of sound tells how loud the sound is. The loudness of a sound is measured in units called decibels. The symbol for decibel is *dB.*

Look at the table to answer these questions.

1. Which sound is the loudest?
2. Which sound is twice as loud as a soft whisper?
3. Which sounds are not as loud as city traffic?
4. How much louder than a subway train is a rock band?

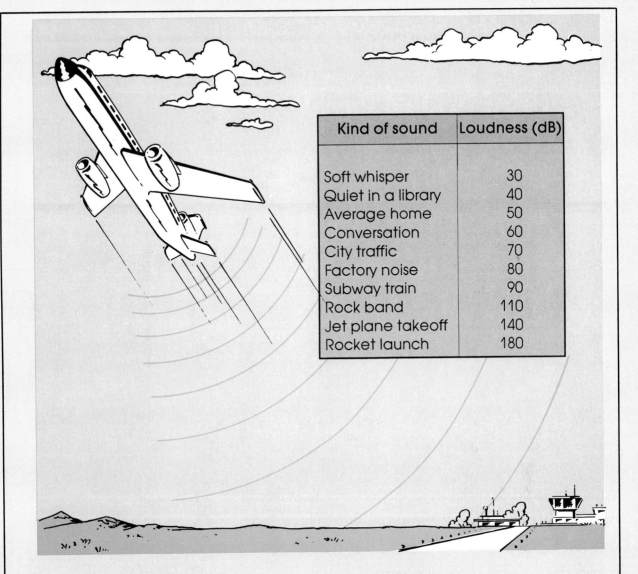

Kind of sound	Loudness (dB)
Soft whisper	30
Quiet in a library	40
Average home	50
Conversation	60
City traffic	70
Factory noise	80
Subway train	90
Rock band	110
Jet plane takeoff	140
Rocket launch	180

MAKING A TABLE

Make a list of the objects in your home that are simple machines. Be sure to look in the kitchen and in places where tools are kept. Many of your toys may be simple machines.

Use this information to make a table. Next to the name of each object, tell what kind of simple machine it is.

Observing Our Earth and Its Neighbors

If you could see the earth from out in space, it would look like a large ball. You live on the earth. And you have probably learned many things about the earth. But there are some things you may not know. You may not know about the inside of the earth. You may not know how the earth is changing. And you may not know about the earth's neighbors in space.

In this unit you will learn many things about the earth. You will also learn about some of the earth's neighbors in space.

Chapter 9

The Changing Earth

How old are you? How have you changed since last year? Perhaps you are taller now. People always change as they get older.

The earth changes, too, as it gets older. Some of these changes take a long time. They may take millions of years.

This picture shows a place that has been changing for a long time. The rock is being worn away. What do you think is causing this change? In this chapter you will learn about some ways the earth changes.

INSIDE THE EARTH
What is it like inside the earth?

In some ways, the earth can be compared to a hard-boiled egg. Look at the drawings of the earth and the egg cut in half. How are they alike? You can see that they both have three layers.

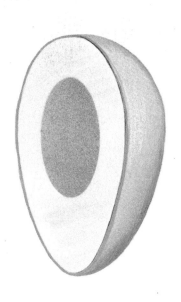

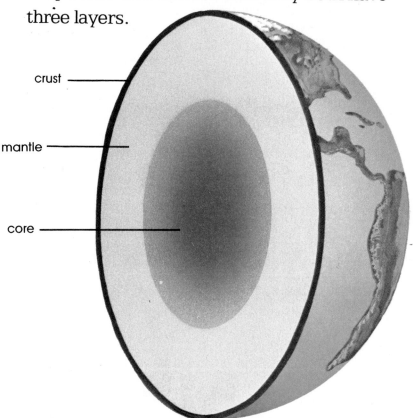

crust ————

mantle ————

core ————

The outer layer of the earth is called the **crust** (krust). Like the eggshell, the crust is the thinnest layer. The crust is made mostly of solid rock. The crust is the most important layer of the earth. You live on the crust.

Using land for farming

Rock outcrop

Food is grown in soil that is part of the crust. Many important materials come from within the crust. Some of these materials are coal, oil, and iron.

Under the earth's crust there is a thicker layer of rocklike material. This layer is called the **mantle** (man′təl). Scientists have never dug into the mantle. But they know it is hot.

The layer beneath the mantle is called the **core** (kôr). Scientists do not think the core is made of rock. They think it is mostly iron. The outer part of the core may be liquid. The center of the core may be solid. The core is the hottest part of the earth.

How can you tell what is inside something without looking?

Materials 3 clay balls / toothpick / compass

Procedure

A. Examine the outside of three clay balls. Each ball may contain a rock, a marble, a metal screw, a piece of wood, a piece of paper, or nothing.
   1. What do you think is inside each ball?

B. Try to find out if there is an object inside each ball. To do this, you may poke a toothpick 15 times into each ball. Be careful not to change the shape of the ball.
   2. Did you find an object in each ball?
   3. What is the size and shape of each object you found?

C. A compass needle is a magnet. Find out if anything inside each ball moves the needle in a compass.

D. Try to guess what is inside each ball.

E. Break apart each ball and look inside.

Conclusion

1. Were you able to find out what was in each ball without looking inside?
2. What else could you have done to find out about the objects?

Using science ideas

What could you do to find out about a present before you open it?

— FAST CHANGES IN THE CRUST —

How do earthquakes and volcanoes change the earth's crust?

The earth's crust is always changing. Some changes are very fast. They may take only a few minutes.

Earthquakes (ėrth'kwāks) cause fast changes in the earth's crust. An **earthquake** is a movement of rock in the crust. This may happen when forces inside the earth push up on the crust. Land may rise or fall when layers of the crust crack and move. Sometimes this movement causes damage at the surface of the crust.

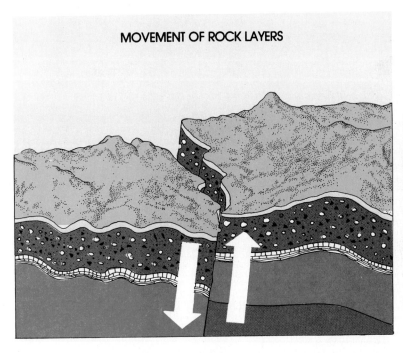

MOVEMENT OF ROCK LAYERS

Earthquake damage

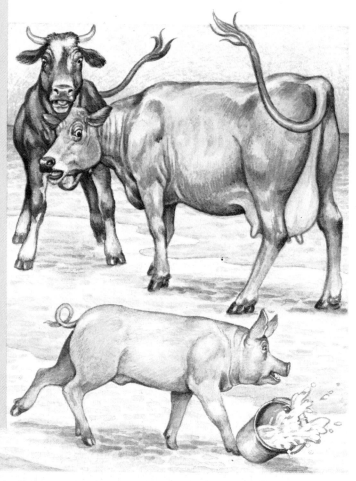

Before an earthquake

It is very hot deep inside the earth's crust. It is hot enough to melt rock. Melted rock is called **magma** (mag′mə). The magma may move up through cracks in the earth's crust. As more and more magma is pushed up to the surface, a volcano (vol kā′nō) is formed. A **volcano** is an opening in the earth's crust through which magma flows.

Here you can see how hot melted rock flows from a volcano. Melted rock that flows from a volcano is called **lava** (lä′və). After lava cools, it hardens into solid rock.

INSIDE A VOLCANO

lava

magma

An active volcano

-SLOWER CHANGES IN THE CRUST-
How are the rocks in the earth's crust changing?

Most people think that anything made of rock will last forever. Rocks may not seem to change. But all rocks on the earth's surface do change. They are worn away. They are slowly broken into smaller pieces. The wearing away and breaking of rock is called **weathering** (weᵀH'ər ing). Most weathering is done by moving water and wind.

Weathered rocks

Stream carrying soil

What happens after rocks are broken into smaller pieces? Some pieces of rock may become part of the soil. Water or wind may carry other pieces to new places. The movement of rock and soil by water and wind is called **erosion** (i rō′zhən).

These pictures show what erosion can do. The stream looks muddy. Soil is being carried to a new place. You can also see land that has been changed by erosion. How will this land look if there is any more erosion?

Eroded land

— CHANGES CAUSED BY WATER —
How does water change the earth's crust?

Have you ever seen the rocks near a river or stream? Most of them are round and smooth. What causes these rocks to become round and smooth?

Fast-moving water in a river or stream can move rocks. The rocks bump into and roll over each other. This causes the sharp edges to break off. In time, the rocks are worn smooth. The water has weathered the rocks.

Rounded rocks

Fast-moving water carries pieces of rock and soil with it. These rocks and soil change the bottom of the river or stream. They cut into it and make it deeper. When the water slows, rocks and soil settle to the bottom. After many years, layers of rock and soil will form new land. Look at the picture. Find the new land that has been formed here.

New land

Water changes rocks in other ways. Sometimes water gets into small holes and cracks in rocks. In cold weather the water can freeze. Water expands as it freezes. Freezing water will make the cracks wider. Soon the rock will start to break into smaller pieces. Freezing water in the cracks of rocks is another way rocks are weathered.

Cracked rocks

How can erosion change rocks?

Materials   rock salt / hand lens / sand / small jar with lid / spoon / water / shallow dish / paper

Procedure

A. Place a few pieces of rock salt on a sheet of paper. Look at the rock salt through a hand lens. Draw what you see.
1. Describe the size and shape of the pieces of rock salt.

B. Put enough rock salt into a jar to cover the bottom. Add a spoonful of sand. Cover the salt and sand with water. Put a lid on the jar.

C. Shake the covered jar for 2 minutes.
2. What do you think is happening to the rock salt?

D. Remove the lid from the jar. Pour the water into a dish. Empty the pieces of rock salt onto the sheet of paper.

E. Look at the rock salt through the hand lens.
3. How has the size and shape of the pieces of rock salt changed?

Conclusion
1. How did erosion change the rock salt?
2. How can moving water and sand in a river or stream change rocks?

Using science ideas
Allow the water in the dish to evaporate. This may take several days. Look at the matter that remains in the dish. Where did the matter come from? How else does moving water change rocks?

— CHANGES CAUSED BY WIND —

How does strong wind change the earth's crust?

Have you ever had dust blown in your face? This may happen on a windy day. Wind may carry pieces of sand and soil.

This picture shows what a dust storm is like. You can see sand and soil being picked up by the wind. Strong winds may blow sand and soil far from where they have been formed. When the winds slow down, these materials are dropped. Sand dunes like these may form. Strong winds cause much weathering and erosion.

A dust storm

Sand dunes

An arch of rock

Sand carried by strong winds can wear away rocks. The moving sand hits the rock. It grinds away bits of the rock. In time the shape of the rock changes. These rocks have been carved by winds that carry pieces of sand.

Sometimes land must be protected from wind. Strong winds may carry away soil that is needed. Land covered with plants will slow down this kind of erosion. The roots of plants hold soil in place.

Wind-carved rocks

— CHANGES CAUSED BY LIVING —
THINGS
How do living things change the crust?

People, plants, and animals live on the earth's crust. Sometimes they change parts of the crust. Perhaps even you have changed some of the crust.

People need roads. The land must be changed when roads are built. Large rocks are broken and moved.

A mountain highway

Digging a foundation

Can you find signs of weathering and erosion?
Look in your yard or neighborhood. Buildings, roads, and sidewalks often show signs of weathering. Look for examples of erosion. You may find places where wind or water is carrying soil or sand away.

Make a chart like this one. It will help you to remember what you have seen. On the chart tell if you have seen weathering or erosion. Tell where it is and what caused it. You may want to make some drawings of what you have seen.

Cracked sidewalk

Tree growing in rock

You may have seen how a tree root can lift and crack a sidewalk. Growing plants can change rocks in the same way. The roots of some plants start to grow in cracks in rocks. As the roots get bigger, the rocks crack more and more. What will happen to this rock as the tree grows?

Some animals move soil and rocks to look for food. They may even live in the soil.

A badger digging

IDEAS TO REMEMBER

▶ The layers of the earth are the crust, the mantle, and the core.

▶ The crust is always changing.

▶ Earthquakes and volcanoes cause fast changes in the earth's crust.

▶ Weathering and erosion cause slower changes in the earth's crust.

▶ The crust is changed by water, wind, and living things.

Reviewing the Chapter

SCIENCE WORDS

A. Copy the sentences below. Use science terms from the chapter to complete the sentences.

1. The wearing away and breaking of rock is called ____.

2. The outer layer of the earth is called the ____.

3. Melted rock inside the earth is called ____.

4. An ____ is a movement of rock in the earth's crust.

5. The movement of rock and soil by water and wind is called ____.

6. The ____ is the hottest part of the earth.

7. A ____ is an opening in the earth's crust through which melted rock flows.

8. The ____ is a layer of rocklike material under the earth's crust.

9 Melted rock that flows from a volcano is called ____.

B. Write as many science terms from the chapter as you can, using the letters in the box. Write a sentence using each term.

C E T
V A
O R N
L S U

UNDERSTANDING IDEAS

A. Write sentences that tell how each of these makes the earth's crust change.

1. earthquake   2. volcano   3. water   4. wind
5. plants   6. animals   7. people

B. Write the term that does not belong in each group.

1. crust, mantle, plant, core
2. lava, wind, magma, volcano
3. wind, ore, water, living things
4. weathering, erosion, earthquake, soil

C. The drawings show some changes in the earth's crust. Write the numbers of the pictures. Next to each number write the cause of the change.

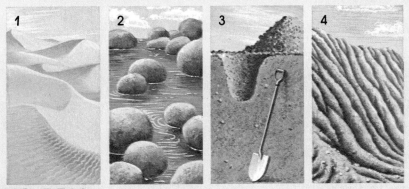

USING IDEAS

1. The earth's crust is changed by water, wind, and living things. Write about two ways in which you have changed the earth's crust.

Chapter 10

The Earth's Resources

Have you ever watched a house being built? If you have, you know that many materials are needed.

In this picture you can see the workers using many different materials. In some way, all of these materials once came from the earth. Name some of the things that came from the earth. Where did the cinder blocks come from? Where did the wood come from?

In this chapter you will learn about many useful things that come from the earth.

SOIL AS A RESOURCE
Why do plants and animals need soil?

Many of the things you need for life come from the earth. You could not live without soil, air, and water. Useful materials from the earth are called **natural resources** (nach'ər əl ri sôr'siz). Soil, air, and water are natural resources.

Soil is a very important natural resource. Plants need soil to grow. People use many kinds of plants for food. People use trees for lumber and to make paper. Every day you use many things that were grown in soil. How many things have you used today that were grown in soil?

Redwood trees

Redwood lumber

Soil is made of many kinds of matter. Most soil is made of pieces of weathered rock. The rock pieces may be very large or as fine as powder.

Most soil has matter that was once living. The remains of dead plants and animals have become part of the soil. When this happens, many useful materials are returned to the soil. Plant and animal matter found in soil is called **humus** (hyü′məs).

Topsoil

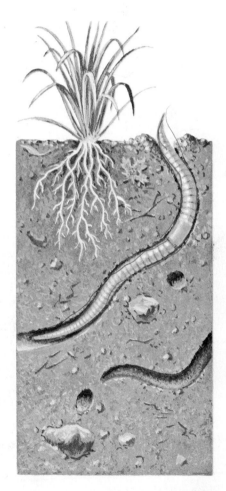

Humus is found in the top layer of soil. This layer of soil is called **topsoil.** Humus helps topsoil to hold water. Plants grow well in topsoil that has a lot of humus.

Sometimes worms live in the soil. Worms use humus for food. Worms make tunnels in the soil. The tunnels allow air and water to move through the soil. Plants need this air and water to grow.

189

Is all soil the same?

Materials 2 paper towels / 2 soil samples / hand lens / 2 small jars with lids / masking tape / pencil / water

Procedure

A. Place two paper towels on your desk. Label one towel *A* and the other towel *B*. Put a sample of soil on each towel.

B. Look at each sample.
   1. How are the two soils alike?
   2. How are the two soils different?

C. Make a chart like the one shown.

Material in soil	Sample A	Sample B
Large rock particles		
Small rock particles		
Plant remains		
Animal remains		

D. Use a hand lens to look for different materials in each sample. Write *yes* or *no* on your chart to answer the following questions.
   3. Which soil has large rock particles?
   4. Which soil has small rock particles?
   5. Which soil has plant and animal remains?

E. Use masking tape to label one jar *A* and the other jar *B*.

F. Put soil sample *A* into jar *A*. Put soil sample *B* into jar *B*. Pour water into the jars so that they are nearly full. Put the lids on tightly. Shake each jar to mix the water and the soil. Wait for the soil in each jar to settle.
   6. What happened to the soil in each jar?

Conclusion

Is all soil the same? Explain your answer.

Using science ideas

In which soil would a plant grow better? Explain.

THE AIR AROUND US

Why is air an important natural resource?

There is air all around you. But you cannot see it. Pure air has no color. You cannot smell pure air. Sometimes you can feel air when it moves. Moving air is called wind. Wind has energy that can make things move. This energy can be used to turn windmills and move sailboats. How else can wind be used?

Windmill

Sailboats

Air is made of many different gases. A gas called nitrogen (ni′trə jən) makes up most of the air. Oxygen (ok′sə jən) is another important gas in the air. Most living things need oxygen. There are also small amounts of other gases in the air.

Do you know?

People and animals use up oxygen from the air when they breathe. Burning things also use up oxygen. The oxygen that is used must be replaced. Living things would die without oxygen.

Green plants make oxygen when they make food. This oxygen is released into the air. Without green plants the oxygen in the air would be used up.

Trees and other green plants are important. Destroying forests and fields can be a threat to our oxygen supply. How would a large forest fire reduce the amount of oxygen in the air?

Rain forest

Pollution from a car

The air around the earth is called the **atmosphere** (at'mə sfir). The atmosphere is not always clean. Winds blow soil into the air. Volcanoes put dust into the air. Many factories put smoke into the air. Cars and trucks add harmful gases to the air.

Anything that makes the air dirty causes **pollution** (pə lü'shən). Air pollution harms many living things. People can become sick from air pollution.

Today many things are being done to control air pollution. Perhaps you can tell what some of these things are.

Mount St. Helens

How do you know there is air pollution?

Materials   3 white cloths / filters from a furnace and a car / hand lens / large sheet of paper

Procedure

A. Use three white cloths to wipe your desk, a bookshelf, and a windowsill.
   1. How do the cloths look now?

B. Examine the cloths with a hand lens. Find the particles of dust.
   2. What do the particles look like?
   3. Where did these particles come from?

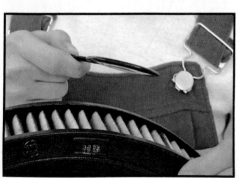

C. Place the filters on a large sheet of paper. Look at the filters with the hand lens. Find the particles of dust.
   4. What do the particles look like?
   5. Where did these particles come from?
   6. Where would these particles go if the filters did not trap them?
   7. Do you think a car would run better with clean air than with polluted air?

Conclusion
Did you find signs of air pollution? Explain.

Using science ideas
Can you think of some things people can do to keep the air clean?

THE EARTH'S WATER SUPPLY

Where can water be found on the earth?

Much of the earth is covered with water. Water is found in oceans, rivers, lakes, and ponds. There may be water in the ground. In some places, water is even found as large pieces of ice. Wherever it is found, water is an important natural resource.

Large iceberg

Shasta Dam and its reservoir

Irrigation

The water that people use comes from many different places. Where there are many people, the water may come from a reservoir (rez'ər vwär). A **reservoir** is a place where water is stored.

Water is needed for farm crops. Most crops get enough water from rain. But in some places there is not enough rain for crops to grow. Farmers must give water to these plants. Giving water to crops when there is not enough rain is called **irrigation** (ir ə gā'shən).

Living things always need water. But sometimes water becomes polluted. This happens when wastes from factories and houses get into the water. Polluted water can harm living things.

Cleaning an oil spill

Removing oil from a duck

How is water cleaned? The water that comes from a reservoir must be cleaned before it can be used. One way to clean water is to filter it.

Make a filter by using a large paper cup and some clean sand. Use a pin to make some holes in the bottom of the cup. Half fill the cup with sand. Hold the cup over a glass to collect the water as it is filtered. Slowly pour some muddy water into the paper cup. Watch as the filtered water drips through the bottom of the cup. What happens to the muddy water as it is filtered?

ENERGY FROM THE EARTH
What kinds of energy come from the earth's crust?

Using gas to cook

Every day you need energy to do many things. You need energy to do work and to play. Your energy comes from the food you eat. Your body uses food as a fuel. A **fuel** is a material that is used to supply energy.

People need many other kinds of energy. Energy is needed to heat homes and to cook food. Energy is needed to move trucks and to run machines.

Fueling a truck

Coal mining and coal   Oil rig and pump

Many fuels are buried in the layers of the earth's crust. Coal, oil, and gas are important fuels that come from the earth's crust. They all give off energy when they are burned. Here you can see how coal is taken from the earth. Oil and gas must be pumped to the surface of the earth.

It took millions of years for coal, oil, and gas to form. These fuels formed from the remains of plants and animals that lived long ago. Fuels are important natural resources.

SOME OTHER RESOURCES
Why are some rocks useful?

You may not think that rocks are useful. But some rocks are. Metals such as iron, copper, gold, and silver are found in rocks. These metals are mixed with other minerals. Rocks that contain metals are called **ores** (ôrz). Mines like this one have been dug to take ores from the earth's crust.

Most of the metals people use come from ores. Coins are made of metal. Most tools and machines are also made of metals.

A copper mine and copper ore

Some rocks are useful because they are strong and beautiful. One of these rocks is marble (mär'bəl). Marble has been used in many buildings.

Marble quarry

Lyndon B. Johnson Library

Sometimes beautiful minerals are found in rocks. These minerals are called **gems** (jemz). Most gems are used to make jewelry. Diamonds (dī'məndz) are one kind of gem.

IDEAS TO REMEMBER

► Natural resources are useful materials that come from the earth.
► Living things need soil, air, and water for life.
► Coal, oil, and gas are used for energy.
► Soil, air, water, fuels, metals, and gems are natural resources.

Diamond

Reviewing the Chapter

SCIENCE WORDS

A. Copy the sentences below. Use science terms from the chapter to complete the sentences.

1. Useful materials from the earth are called ____.
2. Plants grow well in soil that has a lot of ____.
3. The air around the earth is called the ____.
4. A gas called ____ makes up most of the air.
5. People and animals need a gas called ____.
6. Sometimes the water that people use is stored in a ____.
7. Anything that makes air or water dirty causes ____.
8. Watering crops when there is not enough rain is called ____.

B. Find the missing letters for each term. Write a sentence using each term.

1. g _e_ _m_ s   2. _f_ u e _l_
3. _o_ r _e_ s   4. t o _p_ s _o_ i l

UNDERSTANDING IDEAS

A. A *cause* makes things happen. An *effect* is what happens. For each pair of sentences, tell which is the cause and which is the effect.

1. **a.** The air in the atmosphere is not always clean.
   b. Cars and trucks add harmful gases to the air.
2. **a.** Wind has energy that makes things move.
   b. Sailboats move down the river.
3. **a.** Some rocks are used in buildings.
   b. Some rocks are strong and beautiful.
4. **a.** The earth has many natural resources.
   b. Plants and animals can live on earth.

B. Write sentences telling how each of these natural resources is used by people.

   1. soil   **2.** water   **3.** metal   **4.** oil
   5. air   **6.** gas

USING IDEAS

1. Look at old magazines and newspapers. Cut out pictures that show how natural resources are used. Put the pictures into groups for each kind of natural resource. Make a poster to show your pictures.

Chapter 11

The Weather Around You

The weather around you changes from day to day. You may wake up to see the sun shining through your bedroom window. By the time you come home from school it may be raining.

The weather changes in many ways. It can change from warm to cold. It can change from calm to windy. How is the weather in the picture about to change?

In this chapter you will learn about the weather and its changes. You will also learn about what causes the weather to change.

HEATING THE EARTH

How is the earth heated?

You can see that the ice statue is melting even though it is a cold day. It is melting because it is in the sunlight. Have you ever stood in the sun and felt the heat? How do you feel when you walk out of the sunlight and into the shade?

Ice statue

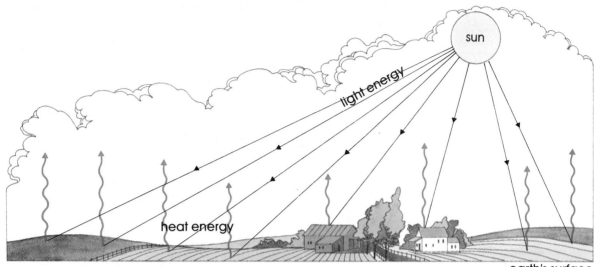

sun

light energy

heat energy

earth's surface

You know that the sun gives off light energy. Some of the light energy travels through space and reaches the earth. When light energy strikes the earth, some of it is changed to heat. The drawing will help you understand how this happens. Have you ever walked barefoot on a beach on a sunny day? If you have, you know the sand felt warm. How did the sand get warm?

The earth is like a giant heater. Heat coming from the earth's surface warms the air above the land. The temperature of the air changes with the amount of sunlight that reaches the earth's surface. The more sunlight the surface gets, the more the air is heated. Why is the air cooler on a cloudy day? Why does it get cooler at night?

Stepping on warm sand

207

SEASONS
What causes the temperature to change with the seasons?

The temperature of many parts of the earth changes with the seasons. These changes are caused by the way light from the sun strikes the earth. Light from the sun strikes the earth differently in winter than it does in summer. Look at the drawings. You can see that during winter, sunlight strikes the earth at a slant. Light striking at a slant spreads out. The ground in this area is heated less at this time of year. In summer, sunlight strikes the earth more directly. This light does not spread out. So the ground gets more heat with direct sunlight.

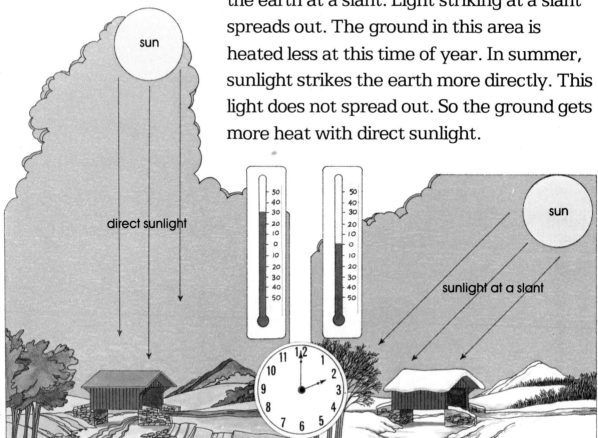

SUMMER

WINTER

The change in seasons is caused by the tilt of the earth as it moves around the sun. Look at the drawing. In summer, the part of the earth where you live is tilted toward the sun. The sunlight strikes the surface more directly. In winter, your part of the earth tilts away from the sun. How does sunlight strike the earth in the winter?

Did you ever notice how much longer the days are in summer than in winter? In winter you may get up when it is still dark outside. In summer you might wake up with the sun in your eyes. There are more hours of daylight in summer than there are in winter. More hours of daylight also cause the earth to become warmer in summer.

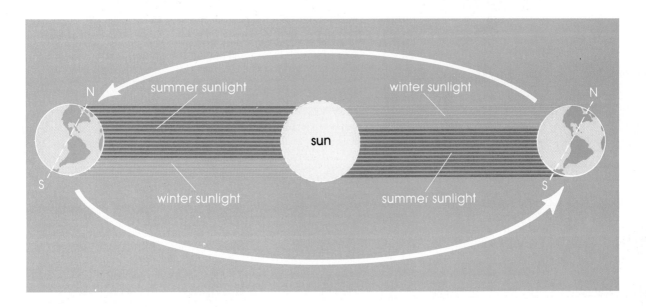

How does the slant of light affect heat?

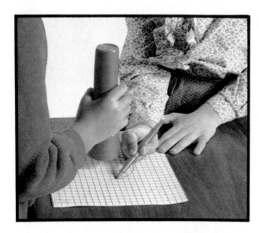

Materials   flashlight / pencil / graph paper

Procedure
A. Hold a flashlight 2 centimeters above a sheet of graph paper. Draw a line around the edge of the outer ring of light.
   1. How many full squares can you count inside the circle?

B. Hold the flashlight at a slant 2 centimeters above the paper. Draw a line around the outer ring of light.
   2. How many full squares can you count inside the circle?
   3. What is the difference in the number of squares in step **A** and step **B**?

Conclusion
1. Did the amount of light change from step **A** to step **B**?
2. Did the amount of space lighted by the flashlight change from step **A** to step **B**?
3. Did each square in step **A** receive more or less light than each square in step **B**?

Using science ideas
At what times during the day would the sun heat the earth's surface least? Why?

— HEATING DIFFERENT SURFACES —
What part of the earth absorbs the most sunlight?

Some energy from the sun changes to heat when it strikes the surface of the earth. The surface of the earth is not the same in all places. Three fourths of the earth is covered by water. The rest of the earth is land. The land changes sunlight to heat faster than the water does. This causes the air over water to be cooler than the air over land during the day.

Light-colored surfaces do not absorb light as well as dark surfaces. When the sun's light strikes light-colored surfaces, much of it bounces off. This light is not changed to heat. The cars in the picture are sitting in the sun. Suppose you could touch each car. Which ones would feel warmest?

Land and water

Light and dark-colored cars

Fields

Many polar regions are covered with snow. Why is the air in these regions cold? Since dark surfaces can absorb more light, they become warmer than light-colored surfaces. The air above dark surfaces also becomes warmer. Which fields in the picture give off the most heat on a sunny day? Why?

Differences in temperature can cause air to move. Warm air is lighter than cold air. Warm air rises when cooler, heavier air moves in and pushes it upward. You can see this happening in the drawing below. The movement of air is called **wind**. Wind helps bring many of the changes in weather.

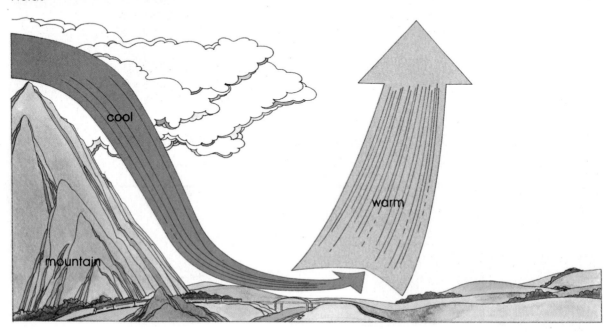

WATER IN THE AIR
How is water changed to a gas?

Energy from the sun does more than heat the earth. It also changes water in lakes, rivers, and oceans. The water is changed to a gas by evaporation. Water in the form of a gas is called water vapor. The particles of water vapor are very small. They are so small that you cannot see them in the air.

Water evaporates faster at some times than at other times. What happens to puddles of water when the sun shines? Will the clothes on the line dry faster if the wind is blowing? Both wind and heat from sunlight speed up the evaporation of water.

Drying clothes

Puddle of water

Water vapor in the air can change back to liquid water. Have you ever seen water on the grass in the morning? This water is called **dew.** It forms when the air and grass become cool. The water vapor in the air changes back to liquid when it touches the cool grass.

Sometimes the temperature of the air drops below freezing. When the air is colder than 0°C, small ice crystals form on the grass. Ice formed in this way is called **frost.** Where else have you seen frost?

Frost

Dew

Finding out

Is there water vapor in the air around you?   Fill a tin can with ice cubes and cold water. Fill another can with warm water. Make sure the water comes to the same level in both cans. Wait 15 minutes. Wipe a finger across the outside of each can. What do you notice? Where does the water come from?

CLOUDS

What happens to water in the clouds?

Warm, moist air gets cooler as it rises. As the air cools, the particles in the air move closer together. When this happens, water vapor is squeezed from the spaces between the air particles. This causes the water vapor to form tiny drops of water on bits of dust. The tiny drops of water are so light that they float in the air. When millions of these drops come together, they form a **cloud.**

There are many kinds of clouds. Some form high in the sky. Others form lower in the sky. The drawing shows three kinds of clouds and where they form.

high clouds (feathery)

middle clouds (fluffy)

low clouds (layered)

Fog

Some clouds are very thick and form in layers. There must be a lot of water vapor in the air for these clouds to form. Other clouds form very high above the ground, where there is not much water vapor in the air. It is below freezing where these clouds form. These clouds are thin and made of ice crystals.

Have you ever walked in a cloud? If you have walked in a fog, you have walked in a cloud. Fog is a cloud close to the ground.

Sometimes clouds gather into thick layers. The wind blows the clouds into cooler air. The drawing shows what happens inside a cloud when the cloud meets cooler air. (1) Small drops of water in clouds come closer together. (2) The small drops join to make

larger and heavier drops. (3) The drops become so heavy that they cannot float in the air. They fall to the ground as rain.

Sometimes the temperature of the air below a cloud is very cold. The rain freezes as it falls. Frozen raindrops are called **sleet.**

During winter the temperature in the clouds may be below freezing. Water vapor in the clouds freezes into tiny crystals of ice. **Snowflakes** form when more water vapor freezes onto the ice crystals. In time the snowflakes fall from the cloud. Snowflakes can be seen in many different shapes. How are these snowflakes different? Snow, rain, and sleet are called **precipitation** (pri sip ə tā'shən).

Snowflakes

Hailstones

WATER CYCLE

What are the steps of the water cycle?

Do you know that water is always moving around you? It is evaporating from bodies of water such as rivers, streams, and oceans. This water rises and cools to form clouds. When clouds cool, tiny drops of water join together and fall to the ground.

One of three things happens to water that falls onto land as rain or snow. (1) Most of it soaks into the ground. (2) Some of it evaporates into the air. (3) Some of its flows into rivers and streams. In time the water in rivers and streams will reach large lakes and oceans. This water evaporates once again into the air. Most of the earth's surface is covered by ocean water. For this reason, most water evaporates from oceans.

The moving of water from the oceans to the air and back to the oceans is called a **water cycle** (sī'kəl). A cycle is something that happens over and over again. A cycle always leads back to where it started. The seasons of the year are another kind of cycle. They happen over and over again. What other cycles can you name?

After a rainstorm

The drawing will help you understand the water cycle. Look at each numbered step as you read.

(1) Energy from the sun changes water to water vapor. (2) Water vapor rises, cools, and condenses to form clouds. (3) Winds blow the clouds over land. (4) Clouds meet cool air, and rain or snow falls to the ground. (5) Most of the water returns to the oceans. The water that returns can now begin the cycle once again.

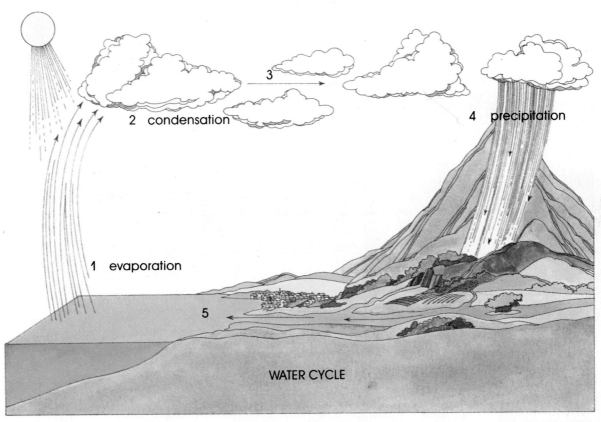

WATER CYCLE

Can you make a water cycle?

Materials   large glass jar / plastic wrap / rubber band / water

Procedure

A. Fill the jar half full of water.

B. Cover the jar with plastic wrap. Hold the plastic wrap in place with a rubber band.

C. Place the jar in a sunny window. Leave it in the window for a few hours.
   1. What do you think will happen inside the jar?

D. Observe what has happened inside the jar.
   2. What do you see on the underside of the plastic wrap?
   3. Where did it come from?
   4. Why did you place the jar in a sunny window?

Conclusion

1. How is what happened inside the jar like the water cycle?
2. Where did evaporation take place?
3. Where did condensation take place?

Using science ideas

How could you speed up the cycle in the jar?

IDEAS TO REMEMBER

▶ The earth is heated by energy from the sun.

▶ Seasons are caused by differences in how sunlight strikes the earth.

▶ Land and dark-colored surfaces absorb more sunlight than water and light-colored surfaces.

▶ Water from the earth's surface evaporates into the air.

▶ Clouds form when water vapor in the air changes to tiny droplets of water.

▶ Precipitation falls from clouds as snow, rain, or sleet.

▶ The water on the earth moves in a cycle.

Reviewing the Chapter

SCIENCE WORDS

A. Write the letter of the term that best matches the definition. Not all the terms will be used.

1. The movement of air
2. Small ice crystals
3. Something that happens over and over again
4. A cloud near the ground
5. Frozen raindrops
6. A name for rain, snow and sleet

    a. precipitation
    b. fog
    c. sleet
    d. dew
    e. frost
    f. wind
    g. cycle

B. Unscramble each group of letters to find a science term from the chapter. Write a sentence using each term.

1. dloucs
2. lasekowfns
3. trewa lycec

UNDERSTANDING IDEAS

A. The sentences describe the water cycle. Write the numbers of the sentences to show the correct order.

  1. Energy from the sun changes water to water vapor.
  2. Most of the water returns to the oceans.
  3. Winds blow the clouds over land.
  4. Water vapor rises and condenses to form clouds.
  5. Clouds meet cool air, and rain or snow falls.

B. Choose one of the drawings to answer each question below.

  1. Which drawing shows the season in which the part of the earth where you live is tilted toward the sun?
  2. Which drawing shows the season in which sunlight strikes the earth at a slant?

USING IDEAS

1. Imagine that you are a weather reporter. Write a report about today's weather.

Chapter 12

Sun, Moon, and Planets

The earth has many neighbors in space. The sun and the moon are important neighbors of the earth. The sun and the moon affect the earth in many ways.

This picture was taken from the moon. The body in space is the earth. You can see that only part of it is lighted by the sun. It is day on the lighted part. It is night on the dark part.

In this chapter you will learn about the sun and the moon. You will also learn about other bodies in space.

— LOOKING AT THE MOON AND — THE SUN

What is it like on the moon and the sun?

Look at the two balls in the first picture. You can see that they are not the same size. Look at the other picture. Each ball is in a different place. The two balls now appear to be the same size. Why is this?

The bodies in space appear smaller than they really are. Sometimes smaller bodies in space look bigger than larger ones.

At night, the moon appears larger than any of the stars in the sky. But the moon is really much smaller than any of the stars. The closer a body in space is, the larger it appears to be. The moon is the earth's closest neighbor in space.

Different-sized balls

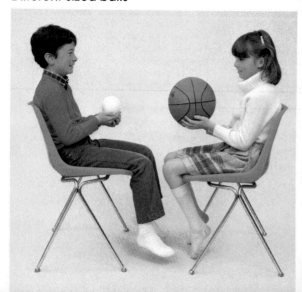

The sun is many times larger than the moon. But it is much farther from the earth than the moon is. Large bodies like the sun look smaller when they are far away.

The moon does not give off its own light. Instead it reflects light from the sun. The sun is the source of light for the earth and the moon.

In some ways the surface of the moon is like the surface of the earth. Both have soil and rocks. Like the earth, the moon has hills and mountains. However, the mountains on the moon are sharper and steeper than those on the earth. They have not been changed by water or wind. Why?

Mountains on the moon

Mountains on the earth

Do you know?

The moon is about 400,000 kilometers from the earth. Suppose you could travel at a speed of 1,000 kilometers an hour. This is the speed of a jet. At this speed it would take you 17 days to reach the moon. It took the astronauts about 3 days to travel to the moon. The sun is much farther from the earth. It would take 150,000 days to reach the sun.

Exploring the moon

When you look at the moon, the mountains are the light-colored areas. Can you find these areas in the picture below?

There are also dark areas on the moon. Find them in the picture. These areas are very smooth. Long ago people thought these areas were large bodies of water. So they called them seas. Today scientists know there is no water on the moon. The dark areas are large flat plains.

The surface of the moon is also marked with craters (krā′tərz). A **crater** is a hollow area that looks like the inside of a bowl. Most scientists think that many of the craters were formed when rocks from space crashed on the surface of the moon.

Areas of the moon

Can you make craters? To do this, you will need some damp sand, several small rocks, a flat pan, and a ruler. Pour the sand into the pan. Make it about 6 centimeters deep. Use the ruler to smooth the surface of the sand. Hold a rock about 20 centimeters above the sand. Drop it into the sand. Do this with the other rocks. Make sure you drop the rocks in different places in the sand. Carefully pick each rock out of the sand. How does the surface of the sand compare with the surface of the moon?

Sun

The sun is like the earth and the moon in shape. But the sun is a much larger ball. The surface of the sun is very different from the surfaces of the earth and the moon. The sun is made of hot, glowing gases. These hot gases are very active. Sometimes they seem to explode from the surface of the sun. In doing this, they form giant streams of gas. These streams of gas are called **sun flares.** They shoot out far into space.

Look at the picture of the sun. Find the sun flare. You can also see light and dark areas on the surface of the sun. These areas show differences in temperature. The light areas are hotter than the dark areas.

MOTIONS IN SPACE

How do the earth and the moon move?

Do you know that you are moving even when you are standing still? You are moving because the earth is moving. The earth is always moving around the sun. A body in space that moves around a larger body is called a **satellite** (sat′ə līt). The earth is a satellite of the sun. The moon is also a satellite. It moves around the earth.

Satellites, like the earth and the moon, always travel in a path around a larger body. This path is called an **orbit** (ôr′bit). In the drawing you can see the earth's orbit around the sun. You can also see the moon's orbit around the earth. Which orbit is longer?

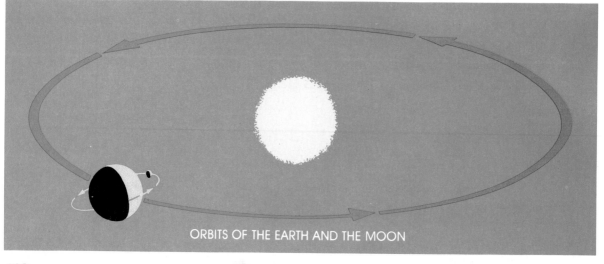

ORBITS OF THE EARTH AND THE MOON

The movement of the earth and the moon in their orbits is called a **revolution** (rev ə-lü'shən). It takes the earth a year to make one revolution around the sun. It takes the moon about a month to make one revolution around the earth.

Most bodies in space also move in another way. They spin. Their spinning motion is like the spinning of a top. The picture of the globe shows how the earth spins. The flag will go around once before it returns to the same position. This full turn is called a **rotation** (rō tā'shən). The earth makes one full rotation every 24 hours. What period of time is 24 hours? Bodies in space rotate at different speeds. The moon rotates only once in about a month.

Spinning a top

Spinning a globe

231

—— PHASES OF THE MOON ——
Why does the moon always look different?

Different moon phases

Have you ever noticed how the shape of the moon seems to change? One night the moon may look full and round. On another night you may see only a small part of the moon. These changes in how the moon looks are called **phases** (fā′ziz).

The moon orbits around the earth about once a month. How much of the moon you can see depends on where the moon is in its orbit around the earth. During the first half of the moon's orbit, more and more of the moon can be seen each night. During the second half, less and less of the moon can be seen. The drawing shows the changes in the position of the moon. Each numbered step shows a different phase of the moon.

1. New moon—The dark side of the moon faces the earth. The moon is in the daytime sky. We cannot see the moon during the new moon phase.

2. First quarter moon—The moon is now one fourth of the way around its orbit of the earth. One half of the lighted side of the moon can be seen from the earth during the first-quarter moon phase.

3. Full moon—The moon is now halfway around its orbit. How much of the lighted half of the moon can you see? After this phase less and less of the moon can be seen each night.

4. Last quarter moon—The moon is now three fourths of the way around its orbit.

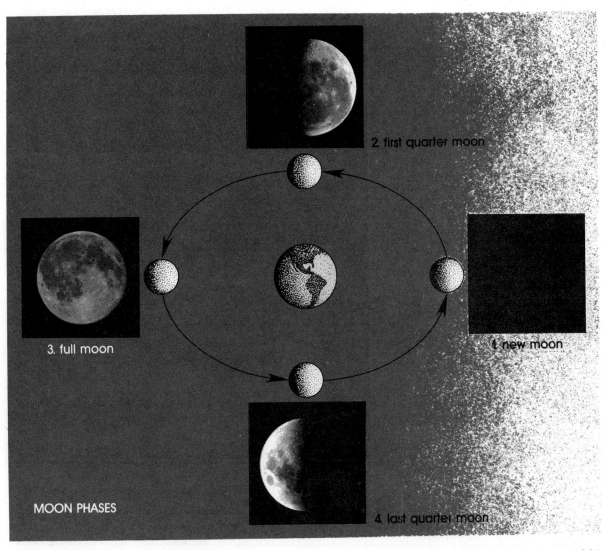

2. first quarter moon

3. full moon

1. new moon

4. last quarter moon

MOON PHASES

ECLIPSES

What is an eclipse?

These children are playing a game. They are trying to see who can make the most unusual shadow. Objects that block the path of light make shadows.

Making shadows

The earth and the moon are large bodies that block the sun's light. In doing so, they make shadows. Sometimes the earth and the moon pass into each other's shadows. When one body passes into the shadow of another, an **eclipse** (i klips') occurs.

At full moon the earth is between the sun and the moon. As the moon orbits the earth, it sometimes enters the shadow the earth makes in space. The drawing shows how the earth's shadow falls on the moon. When this happens, the moon does not get light from the sun. The moon seems to disappear into the shadow. This is called an **eclipse of the moon.**

At new moon the moon is between the sun and the earth. Sometimes the moon blocks the sun's light from part of the earth. The drawing shows how the moon's shadow falls on the earth. This is an **eclipse of the sun.** You can see that the moon's shadow only falls on a small area of the earth. Where must you be to see an eclipse of the sun?

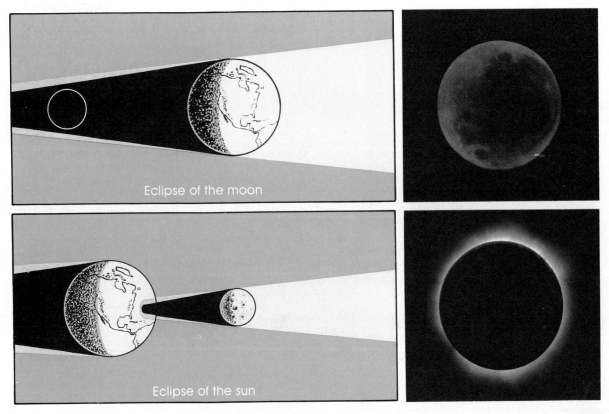

Eclipse of the moon

Eclipse of the sun

How do eclipses take place?

Materials   globe / flashlight / small ball

Procedure

A. Work with a partner. Place a globe on a table. Stand one meter from the globe and hold a flashlight.

B. Darken the room and turn on the flashlight. The light should be shining on the globe.
   1. What does the flashlight represent?

C. Have your partner hold a small ball between the globe and the flashlight. You should be able to see a shadow on the globe.
   2. What does the ball represent?
   3. What part of the globe is in the shadow?
   4. What would you see if you were in the shadow?
   5. What kind of eclipse does this represent?

D. Now place the ball behind the globe.
   6. Does the ball receive any light in this position?
   7. What kind of eclipse does this represent?
   8. Where would you have to be to see this kind of eclipse?

Conclusion

1. During what phase of the moon does an eclipse of the sun take place?
2. During what phase of the moon does an eclipse of the moon take place?
3. How is an eclipse of the sun like an eclipse of the moon?
4. How is an eclipse of the sun different from an eclipse of the moon?

THE PLANETS
What are planets?

The earth is not the only body that revolves around the sun. Other large bodies revolve around the sun. They are called **planets** (plan'its). There are nine planets. The earth, the other planets, and the sun are all part of a large system. This system is called the **solar system** (sō' lər   sis'təm).

You can see the sun and the planets in the drawing. Each planet has its own orbit around the sun. Which planet is nearest the

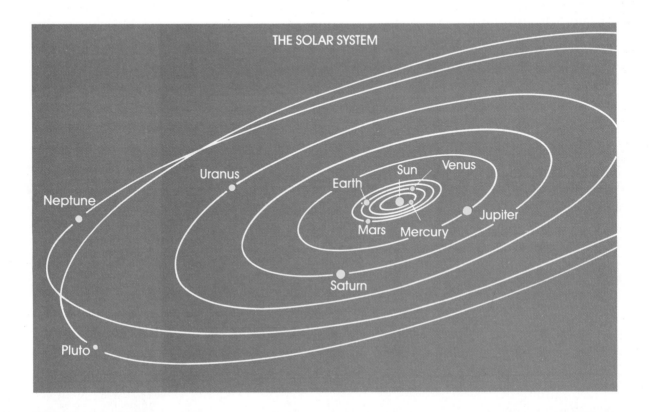

THE SOLAR SYSTEM

Neptune

Uranus

Earth

Sun

Venus

Mars Mercury

Jupiter

Saturn

Pluto

How do the planets move?

Materials paper / crayon / hole punch / string

Procedure

A. The students in your class will act as parts of a solar system model. There will be nine planets, one moon, and one sun.

B. Use a crayon to write the name of your part in the model. Print the name in large letters on a piece of paper.

C. Use a hole punch to make two holes in the paper. Put a piece of string through the holes. Tie the string to make a loop. Hang the sign around your neck.

D. Your teacher will tell you where to stand and how to move.

E. The planets should all walk around the sun at the same speed. The moon walks around the earth as it moves. Everyone will stop walking when the earth is back where it started. It takes the earth a year to go around the sun once.

Conclusion

1. A year is the time it takes a planet to go around the sun once. Each planet's year is different. Which planet has the shortest year? Which planet has the longest year?

2. Which planets did not make a complete orbit around the sun during one earth year?

3. Which planets completed more than one orbit around the sun during one earth year?

sun? Which planet is farthest away from the sun? Mercury (mėr′kyər ē) and Venus (vē′nəs) are closer to the sun than the earth is. These planets are also hotter than the earth. Mars (märz), Jupiter (jü′pə tər), Saturn (sat′ərn), Uranus (yür′ə nəs), Neptune (nep′tün), and Pluto (plü′tō) are farther from the sun than the earth. The farther a planet is from the sun, the colder it is on that planet. Which planet is the coldest?

Saturn

IDEAS TO REMEMBER

▶ The surfaces of the earth, the moon, and the sun are different from each other.

▶ The earth and the moon revolve and rotate.

▶ Changes in how the moon looks from the earth are called phases.

▶ An eclipse takes place when the earth or the moon passes into the other's shadow.

▶ The sun and the planets make up the solar system.

Reviewing the Chapter

SCIENCE WORDS

A. Copy the sentences below. Use science terms from the chapter to complete the sentences.

1. A body in space that moves around a larger body is called a ＿＿.
2. The path on which the earth travels around the sun is an ＿＿.
3. The movement of the moon around the earth is a ＿＿.
4. The spinning motion of the earth is called a ＿＿.
5. When the earth or the moon passes into the other's shadow, an ＿＿ occurs.
6. The sun and the planets make up the ＿＿.

B. Write the letter of the term that best matches the definition. Not all the terms will be used.

1. Hollow areas on the moon's surface
2. Giant streams of gas from the sun
3. Changes in how the moon looks
4. Bodies that orbit the sun
5. Path of a satellite

a. phases
b. orbit
c. sun flares
d. craters
e. eclipse
f. planets

UNDERSTANDING IDEAS

A. Write *T* for the sentences that are true and *F* for the sentences that are false.

1. The earth is a satellite of the moon.
2. The dark areas on the moon are plains.
3. The earth and the moon revolve and rotate.
4. The earth makes one revolution every 24 hours.
5. The moon is smaller than any of the stars.
6. The moon reflects the light of the sun.

B. Explain the difference between an eclipse of the sun and an eclipse of the moon.

USING IDEAS

You can map and measure the location of the planets. To do this, you need a metric ruler, a meter stick, and adding machine tape. Use a piece of tape 4 m long. One end of the tape should be marked "sun." Make a mark 4 cm from the sun. This is the location of Mercury. Make a mark for each planet using the table. Label the location of each planet.

Planet	Distance from the End of Tape
Mercury	4 cm
Venus	7 cm
Earth	10 cm
Mars	15 cm
Jupiter	52 cm
Saturn	95 cm
Uranus	192 cm
Neptune	300 cm
Pluto	395 cm

Science in Careers

Everyone needs and uses materials from the earth. *Farmers* and *ranchers* use the soil to grow food.

Soil scientists study soil to find ways to make it better.

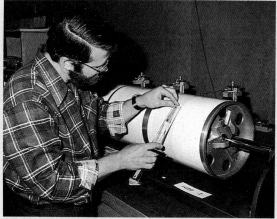
Seismologist

Soil scientist

Geologists (jē ol'ə jists) study the earth's crust. They look for oil, minerals, and other natural resources.

Chemists find ways to use materials from the crust.

Seismologists (sīz mol'ə jists) study earthquakes. They try to find out what the inside of the earth is like.

Astronomers (ə stron'ə mərz) and *astronauts* (as'trə nôts) are space scientists. They explore space, using telescopes or spacecraft. They study the sun, moon, stars, and other bodies in space.

Astronaut

People in Science

Hugo Benioff (1899–   )

Hugo Benioff is a scientist who studied the shock waves produced by earthquakes. He designed and built instruments to measure the shock waves. The instruments are called seismographs (sīz′mə grafs). Earthquakes occur along cracks in the crust of the earth. Benioff showed how shock waves caused by an earthquake are related to the size of the crack.

The San Andreas Fault in California

Developing Skills

WORD SKILLS

A compound word is made up of two or more words. Each word has a different meaning. When the words are put together, the new compound word has another meaning. For example, the words *water* and *fall* together make the compound word *waterfall.*

Make compound words by matching words from group **A** with words from group **B.**

A	
earth	sun
air	work
water	light
moon	flood
chalk	wind

B	
plane	house
proof	beam
fall	quake
flow	board
light	bench

READING A TABLE

The table on the next page lists the planets. The table also shows the time it takes for each planet to orbit the sun and the number of satellites each planet has.

Use the table to answer these questions.

1. How long does it take the earth to make one orbit?

2. Which planet has the shortest orbit?

3. Suppose you went to Saturn today. How old would you be after one orbit was made?

4. Which planet has as many satellites as the earth?

5. How many more satellites does Jupiter have than Neptune?

Planet	Length of One orbit	Number of Satellites
Mercury	88 days	0
Venus	225 days	0
Earth	365 days	1
Mars	2 years	2
Jupiter	12 years	16
Saturn	30 years	22
Uranus	84 years	5
Neptune	165 years	3
Pluto	248 years	1

MAKING A TABLE

The temperature of the air outside changes from day to day. There are many ways you can find out what the air temperature is. You may look at a thermometer. You may listen to a radio or TV weather report.

Make a table to show the temperature for a week or longer. Make sure to find out the temperature at the same time each day. Make a column to show if it was sunny, cloudy, or rainy.

Look over the information in the table. Does your table show that the temperature got higher each day? Or does it show that the temperature got lower each day?

Observing Your Health

Good health is important all your life. But good health does not just happen by itself. There are many things you can do to stay healthy. Look at the pictures. What are these people doing to stay healthy? What other things can you do to stay healthy?

In this unit you will learn about some things you can do to keep good health. If you learn to do these things, they can help you lead a better life.

Chapter 13

Good Health Habits

You can do many things to keep your body healthy. When your body is healthy, it works the way it should. You feel good. Knowing what to do to keep your body healthy can keep you from becoming sick. The things you learn now about having a healthy body will be important all your life.

In this chapter you will learn about keeping your body clean. You will learn why exercise and rest are important. You will also learn about safety while riding a bicycle. The things you learn in this chapter should become part of your good health habits.

— KEEPING YOURSELF CLEAN —

What are some ways of keeping your body clean?

Do you do certain things each day without thinking about them? Things that we do without having to think about them are called **habits** (hab′its). People have good habits and bad habits. To be healthy, you should practice good health habits.

One good health habit is to keep yourself clean. Being clean helps keep germs (jėrmz) away. **Germs** are harmful living things that can make people sick. They are too small to see.

One way to be clean is to wash your hands with soap and water before you eat. Washing with soap and water helps to keep

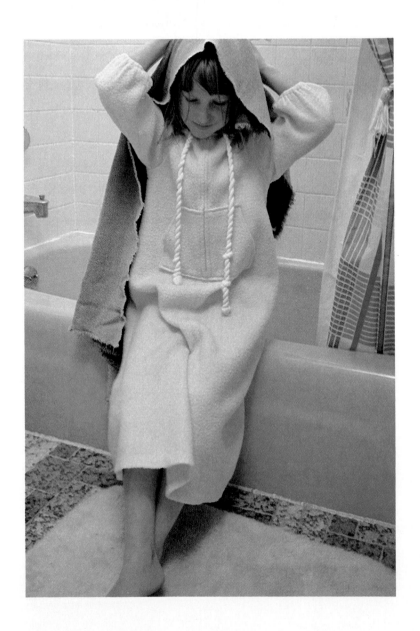

germs from getting in your food. Do you
always wash your hands before you eat?

Taking a bath or shower is another way to
be clean. Do you take a bath or shower
every day? After a bath or shower you will
feel and smell clean.

Another way to be clean is to wash your hair. Some people wash their hair every day. Others wash their hair only once a week. You should wash your hair with shampoo.

After you wash your hair, you should dry it and brush it. Brushing your hair makes it soft and shiny. Brushing your hair between washings also helps to keep it healthy.

Do you know?

You know that you wash your body and hair to remove germs. How are germs kept out of your eyes? You wash around your eyes with soap and water. But your eyes are washed by tears. Each time you blink, tears are spread across your eyes. When a speck of dirt gets in your eye, it is usually washed out by tears. Tears help to keep germs away from the eyes, too. Making tears is your body's way of keeping your eyes clean.

How does soap break up oil?

Materials small jar or other container / medicine dropper / cooking oil / liquid soap / spoon

Procedure

A. Fill a jar almost to the top with cold water. Using a medicine dropper, add three drops of oil. Move the jar gently in a small circle.
    1. How does the oil look?
    2. What happens to the oil?

B. Add three drops of liquid soap to the water and oil. Stir with a spoon.
    3. What happens to the oil?

C. Empty the jar. Then fill it almost to the top with warm water. Add three drops of oil to the warm water.
    4. Does the oil look different in warm water than it did in cold water?

D. Add three drops of liquid soap to the warm water and oil. Stir with a spoon.
    5. What happens to the oil?

Conclusion

1. What happens to oil when it is mixed with water?
2. How does soap break up oil?

Using science ideas

1. Shampoo is a soap used for washing hair. What happens to oil in water when shampoo is added to the water?
2. Why should you use shampoo when you wash your hair?

TEETH CARE

How can you take good care of your teeth?

Your teeth are very important to you. Learning to take care of your teeth now will help prevent problems when you are older. It is best to brush your teeth after every meal and before bedtime.

It is important to brush your teeth properly. You should always use a good toothbrush. Many dentists say you should brush your teeth with short back-and-forth strokes. The brush should be held gently against the teeth. The pictures show where to place a toothbrush when brushing the different surfaces of your teeth.

Brushing your teeth helps to remove bits of food from spaces between the teeth. It

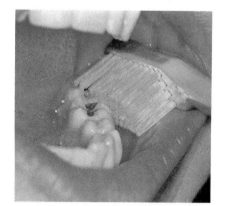

Brushing outside back teeth

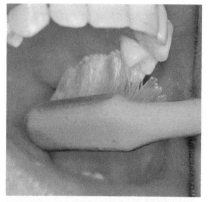

Brushing inside back teeth

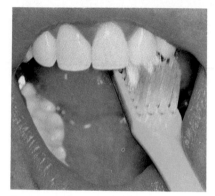

Brushing inside front teeth

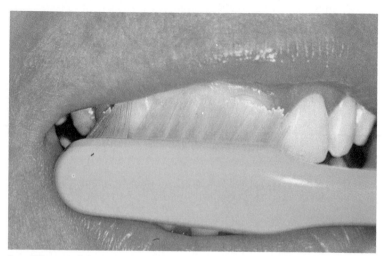

Brushing outside front teeth

also removes plaque (plak) from teeth. **Plaque** is a sticky film made up of tiny germs. It causes teeth to decay. A tooth decays when the tiny germs in plaque change certain foods into a harmful substance. The harmful substance can make a hole in the outside covering of a tooth. A hole in a tooth is called a **cavity** (kav′ə tē). If a cavity is not repaired by a dentist, it may become larger.

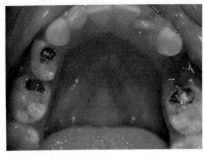
Cavities in teeth

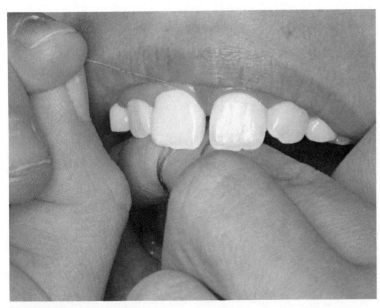
Flossing teeth

Brushing often does not remove all the food and plaque from your teeth. A special kind of thread called **dental floss** (flôs) must be used. The picture shows how teeth are flossed. You should floss your teeth once a day.

255

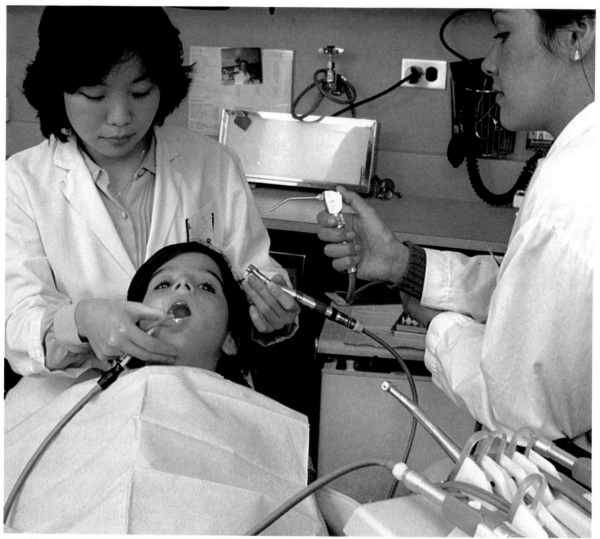
Dentist cleaning teeth

A dentist can help you keep your teeth healthy. By having a checkup you can make sure little problems do not become big problems. The dentist can clean your teeth and repair cavities. When you visit your dentist ask about the best way to take care of your teeth.

EXERCISE AND SLEEP

Why are exercise and rest important to your health?

Regular exercise is important to your health. Exercise makes your body work hard. Exercise keeps the muscles (mus′əls) in your body strong. Muscles that are well exercised can work longer without getting tired. Exercise also makes your heart stronger.

You can get exercise in many different ways. You can walk or ride a bicycle. You can jump rope or swim. You can play games such as softball.

An exercise class

Jumping rope

You should exercise every day for at least 15 minutes. Exercise will then become a good health habit. You should begin exercising slowly. This way you will not hurt your muscles.

You can exercise by yourself. Some exercises you can do by yourself are walking, running, or jumping rope. You can also exercise by playing games with your friends. You can play soccer or volleyball. You can run races with your friends.

Your body needs rest as well as exercise. Sometimes you rest by sitting still. When you are very tired, you usually sleep. You may even take a nap during the day if you are tired.

Your body needs some sleep every day. When you sleep, your body does not work hard. Your breathing slows down and your heart beats more slowly. Sleep gives your body a chance to repair itself. It also allows your mind to rest. Without sleep, your body becomes tired and worn-out. Then you might get sick.

People need different amounts of sleep. Some people need more sleep than others. Small babies sleep about 20 hours a day. You probably sleep 8 to 10 hours a day. Older people need only about 6 hours of sleep a day. You know you have had enough sleep if you wake up feeling rested. How many hours of sleep do you get each day?

What are some stretching exercises?

Materials   none

Procedure

A. Do this exercise. Stand up straight with your arms at your side. Spread your feet a little. Move your head in a circle from right to left three times. Try to make your chin touch your chest. Now move your head in a circle from left to right three times.

    1. What muscles are you stretching?

B. Do another exercise. Stand up straight with your feet apart. Raise both arms over your head. Stand on your toes and reach as high as you can. Hold this position while you count to five. Do this three times.

    2. What muscles are you stretching?

C. Do the exercise shown in the pictures. Stand up straight with your feet apart. Hold your arms straight out at your side. Keep your arms and legs straight as you bend to touch your toes. Touch the toes on your left foot with your right hand. Then come back to your starting position. Now touch the toes on your right foot with your left hand. Do this exercise three times.

    3. What muscles are you stretching?

Conclusion

1. How do stretching exercises help your muscles?

2. How do your muscles feel after stretching?

SAFETY HABITS

How do safety habits help you to stay healthy?

Safety is an important part of staying healthy. Good safety habits help prevent accidents that might hurt you.

You should be very careful when you ride a bicycle. You are riding safely if you do these things.

- Watch out for cars and people.
- Watch for rocks and holes in the street.
- Obey all traffic signals.
- Follow the same traffic rules that people driving cars do.
- Ride in the same direction in which traffic is moving.
- Ride next to the curb.
- Ride on bicycle paths whenever possible.

Riding safely

Stopping at an intersection

Many bicycle accidents can be prevented. Most can be prevented if you make sure that drivers of cars can see you. Always wear light-colored clothing when you ride. A flag on your bicycle also makes you easier to see in the daytime. In dim light, reflectors on your bicycle will help drivers to see you. Your bicycle should have reflectors on the front and back wheels. You should also have reflectors on the pedals. When you ride with a friend, always ride in single file. Be sure to use hand signals before you stop or make a turn. If you follow these rules, bicycle riding will be fun and safe.

Finding out

Do you practice good health habits? At the end of the day, answer these questions about yourself. Do this for a week. Keep a record of your answers in a notebook. At the end of the week, look at all your answers. What can you do to improve your health habits?

1. I exercised today.   Yes   No
2. I brushed my teeth after every meal.   Yes   No
3. I rested today.   Yes   No
4. I took a bath or shower today.   Yes   No
5. I used hand signals when I rode my bicycle today.   Yes   No
6. I washed my hands before meals today.   Yes   No

Bicycle inspection

IDEAS TO REMEMBER

▶ Good health habits help you to stay healthy.

▶ Keeping yourself clean helps keep germs away.

▶ Taking care of your teeth can prevent cavities.

▶ Exercise keeps muscles in your body strong.

▶ Getting enough rest is important for good health.

▶ Practicing good safety habits will help keep you healthy.

Reviewing the Chapter

SCIENCE WORDS

A. Use all the terms below to complete the sentences.

germs　　plaque　　cavity　　dental floss

Learning to care for your teeth is important. Brushing helps to remove bits of food and __1__ from teeth. A special kind of thread called __2__ can also be used to clean teeth. A tooth decays when tiny __3__ in plaque change certain foods into a harmful substance. The harmful substance will make a hole in the outside covering of the tooth. This hole is called a __4__ .

B. Unscramble each group of letters to find a science term from the chapter. Write a sentence using each term.

1. batihs　　**2.** stinted　　**3.** serexiec　　**4.** ayseft

UNDERSTANDING IDEAS

A. A *cause* makes things happen. An **effect** is what happens. For each pair of sentences, write which is the cause and which is the effect.

1. **a.** You do not get enough sleep.
   b. Your body is tired and worn out.
2. **a.** You exercise every day.
   b. The muscles in your body can work longer.
3. **a.** You have few cavities.
   b. You brush your teeth properly.

B. Explain why exercise and rest are important to your health.

C. List three good health habits you should practice in taking care of your teeth.

USING IDEAS

1. Use two or three sheets of drawing paper to make a booklet. On each page, draw a picture of yourself practicing a good health habit. Draw a picture on the cover. Think of a title for your booklet.
2. Make a health or safety poster. Choose one or more good health or safety habits for your poster. Think of a title for your poster.

Chapter 14

Nutrition

Did you ever hear someone say, "You are what you eat"? The food that you eat really becomes part of you. This is why eating good food is important. Some foods give your body the energy it needs. Other foods are important for keeping muscles and bones strong. Some foods help your body to grow and to repair itself. How do you know which foods to eat? Which foods are healthful and which are not?

In this chapter you will learn why food is so important for your body. You will learn about the different kinds of food you eat. You will also learn how to have good eating habits.

THE NEED FOR FOOD

Why do you need to eat food?

The food you eat is important to your body in many ways. Food provides the energy you need for everything you do. You are using energy while you are reading this book. You use a lot more energy when you jump rope or run. You even use energy when you sleep. This energy comes from food.

There is energy in all foods. But some foods have more energy than others. The

Using less energy

Using more energy

Raisins

Apple

Honey

Swimming

Nuts

pictures show foods that have a lot of energy. Some foods with a lot of energy are potatoes, bread, raisins, fruit, and cheese. You should eat foods like these when you are very active. When you are not very active, you are not using as much energy. You should eat foods that do not have as much energy. Vegetables such as lettuce and tomatoes have less energy than the foods in the pictures.

Cheese

KINDS OF FOOD
How are nutrients used by your body?

Your body uses many kinds of food. The food you eat contains many things. The parts of food that help your body grow and give you energy are **nutrients** (nü′trē ənts). There are six main kinds of nutrients. They are (1) sugar and starch, (2) fat, (3) protein (prō′tēn), (4) vitamins (vī′tə mins), (5) minerals, and (6) water.

Sugar and **starch** give your body quick energy. Apples, bananas, oranges, honey, and other sweet foods contain sugar. Bread, potatoes, and noodles have starch. All these foods give you the energy you need to work and play. Sugar and starch that are not used for energy are stored as fat.

Using quick energy

Some quick-energy foods

Fat also has a lot of energy. Fat has more than twice as much energy as sugar or starch. Your body stores the fat that it does not use. This stored fat can be used when your body needs extra energy. Stored fat also helps to keep your body warm. Having too much fat stored in your body is not healthy. Butter, cheese, nuts, and milk have fat. All the foods in the picture have fat.

Measuring growth

Some foods that contain fat

Protein is needed for your muscles, bones, and other body parts to grow. While you are young and growing, you need lots of protein. The boy in the picture needs the foods shown to grow. Since you cannot store protein, you should eat foods that have protein every day. Meat, eggs, beans, and cheese are foods that have protein.

Some protein foods

271

Minerals also are needed for growth. They help your body rebuild worn-out parts as well. Certain minerals help build strong bones and teeth. They are found in milk, cheese, and vegetables. Iron is an important mineral. It is important for healthy blood. Iron is found in liver and green vegetables.

Vitamins help your body to work the way it should. You need many different kinds of vitamins. Most vitamins are named after letters of the alphabet. All foods have vitamins. There is more than one kind of vitamin B. Leafy vegetables, eggs, and milk have some of the B vitamins. The vitamin B

Do you know?

Some people do not eat meat. These people are vegetarians (vej ə tār'ē əns). Their meals are mostly made up of vegetables. They get the nutrients they need without eating meat, fish, or chicken. By choosing the right foods, it is possible to get enough protein without eating meat. Other foods rich in protein are cheese, eggs, peanut butter, dried beans, and nuts.

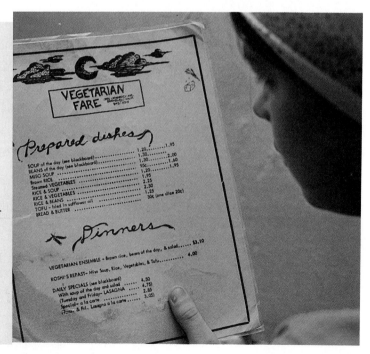

group is important for growth and energy. Oranges and other fruits have vitamin C that helps to keep you healthy. Vitamin D in milk helps your teeth and bones stay strong.

Water is a very important nutrient. You should drink six to eight glasses of water every day. Some of the water you need is found in milk or fruit juice. There is also a lot

of water in some fruits and vegetables. You cannot live without water. Over half your body is made of water.

It is important that you have all six kinds of nutrients each day. But how can you tell if the foods you eat have all the nutrients you need? One way to find out is to read the labels on boxes, cans, or jars of foods. The labels list the nutrients in the foods.

NUTRITION INFORMATION

SERVING SIZE: 1 OZ. (28.4 g. ABOUT ½ CUP) CEREAL ALONE OR WITH ½ CUP VITAMIN D FORTIFIED WHOLE MILK.
SERVINGS PER PACKAGE: 12

| | FLAKES OF WHOLE CORN | |
	CEREAL	WITH MILK
CALORIES	110	180
PROTEIN	2 g	6 g
CARBOHYDRATE	24 g	30 g
FAT	1 g	5 g
SODIUM	185 mg	245 mg

PERCENTAGE OF U.S. RECOMMENDED DAILY ALLOWANCES (U.S. RDA)

| | FLAKES OF WHOLE CORN | |
	CEREAL	WITH MILK
PROTEIN	4	10
VITAMIN A	25	30
VITAMIN C	25	25
THIAMIN	25	30
RIBOFLAVIN	25	35
NIACIN	25	25
CALCIUM	*	15
IRON	4	6
VITAMIN D	10	25
VITAMIN E	25	25
VITAMIN B$_6$	25	30
FOLIC ACID	25	25
VITAMIN B$_{12}$	25	30
PHOSPHORUS	6	20
MAGNESIUM	6	10
ZINC	25	30
COPPER	4	4

*CONTAINS LESS THAN 2% OF THE U.S. RDA OF THIS NUTRIENT.

INGREDIENTS LISTED IN ORDER OF PREDOMINANCE.
INGREDIENTS: WHOLE CORN KERNELS, MALT FLAVORING, SALT, BAKING SODA.

FORTIFIED WITH: VITAMIN C (SODIUM ASCORBATE AND ASCORBIC ACID), VITAMIN E (VITAMIN E ACETATE), NIACIN (NIACINAMIDE), ZINC (ZINC OXIDE), VITAMIN A (VITAMIN A PALMITATE), VITAMIN B$_6$ (PYRIDOXINE HYDROCHLORIDE), VITAMIN B$_2$ (RIBOFLAVIN), VITAMIN B$_1$ (THIAMIN HYDROCHLORIDE), FOLIC ACID, VITAMIN B$_{12}$ AND VITAMIN D$_2$.

Food label

What nutrients are in food?

Materials food labels from 4 or more different foods

Procedure

A. Look at the food label in the picture on page 273.

    1. Does the food contain protein?

    2. Does the food contain carbohydrates (sugar or starch)?

    3. What other nutrients does the food contain?

B. Make a chart like the one shown. The first line has been filled in as an example. The information is from the food label on page 273.

Food	Protein	Fat	Carbohydrates (sugar and starch)	Vitamins	Minerals
Cereal	✓	✓	✓	✓	✓

C. Look at food labels from four or more different foods. Fill in your chart with the information from the labels.

    4. Which food has the most nutrients?

    5. Which food has the fewest nutrients?

Conclusion

1. What nutrients are in foods? How do you know?

2. What other information about a food can you find out by reading the food label?

FOOD GROUPS

What are the four main food groups?

Your **diet** (dī′ət) is all the food you eat. You know that food has nutrients. If you are getting all the nutrients your body needs, you are eating a balanced diet. A balanced diet includes foods from each of the four food groups. The four food groups are (1) meats, (2) breads and cereals, (3) fruits and vegetables, and (4) milk products.

The meat group is made up of foods that have a lot of protein. Chicken, fish, meat, eggs, nuts, and dried beans are in this group.

Foods from the four food groups

You should eat at least two servings from the meat group every day.

The bread and cereal group is made up of foods that have a lot of starch. Rice, noodles, cereal, and bread are in this group. You should eat four or more servings from the bread and cereal group every day.

The fruit and vegetable group is made up of foods that have sugar, starch, minerals, and vitamins. The group includes all fruits and vegetables. You should eat at least four servings from this group every day.

The milk group is made up of foods that have vitamins, minerals, protein, and some fat. All the foods in this group come from milk. They include cheese, butter, and ice

Finding out

What is the diet of other people like? People in other parts of the world eat foods that are different from the foods you eat. Children in Japan might eat rice with vegetables and fish for lunch. Children in Jamaica (jə mā′kə) might eat black beans with pork and coconut for lunch.

Look in cookbooks and other books to find out what foods people in other countries eat. Do they eat foods from the four food groups?

cream. You should eat three servings from this group every day.

You should eat some foods from each group at every meal. The pictures show a balanced breakfast, lunch, and dinner. Can you tell which group each food comes from? If you eat food from each group every day, you will have a balanced diet.

Breakfast

Dinner

Lunch

What foods are in a balanced diet?

Materials   old magazines and newspapers / scissors / 3 large pieces of paper / paste / crayons

Procedure

A. Look through magazines and newspapers for pictures of food. Cut out the pictures.

B. Choose foods from the pictures to make a balanced breakfast. Paste the pictures on a piece of paper. If you cannot find pictures for certain foods, use crayons to draw them.
  1. What food groups are in your breakfast?
  2. What food groups are missing?

C. Repeat step **B,** but this time choose pictures to make a balanced lunch.
  3. What food groups are in your lunch?
  4. What food groups are missing?

D. Repeat step **B** again, this time choosing pictures to make a balanced dinner.
  5. What food groups are in your dinner?
  6. What food groups are missing?

Conclusion

1. How many servings from each food group are in the meals you planned?
2. What is a balanced diet?
3. What foods are in a balanced diet?

Using science ideas

Plan a balanced meal for a very active person. Plan another balanced meal for a person who is not active. How are the meals different?

── HEALTHY EATING HABITS ──
What are three healthy eating habits?

You know that you should eat three balanced meals a day. If you get hungry between meals, you should choose a snack from one of the four food groups. Snacks that are not good for you are foods with a lot of sugar and fat. They do not give you vitamins and minerals. Potato chips, cake, candy, and soft drinks are not good snack foods. What are some good snack foods?

The pictures show some snacks that are good for you. What food groups do these foods come from? Snacks that are good for you are part of a balanced diet. Eating a balanced diet is a healthy eating habit.

Cereal with milk

Peanut butter and celery

Cheese and crackers

Fresh foods

Another healthy eating habit is to eat fresh foods. Fresh foods are sometimes called natural foods. Fresh foods often have more vitamins and minerals than foods in cans, jars, or boxes.

You should eat only as much food as your body needs. If you eat more food than your body needs, the unused food will be stored as fat. By eating too much food, you may gain too much weight. If you do not eat enough food, your body cannot get the energy it needs. You may feel tired. You may lose weight. A doctor can tell you if you should gain or lose weight. A general rule is to eat only at mealtimes and only until you are full. And be sure to eat a balanced diet.

Look at the picture. You can see people playing basketball. What should be the eating habits of these people?

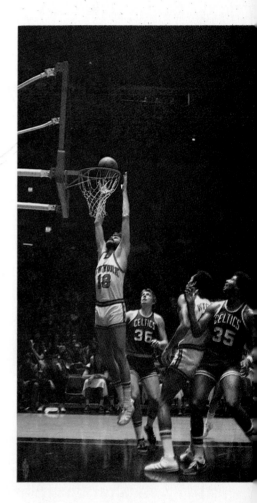

IDEAS TO REMEMBER

▶ Food is the source of energy for everything you do.
▶ The six kinds of nutrients are sugar and starch, fat, protein, vitamins, minerals, and water.
▶ Vitamins help to keep your body working the way it should.
▶ Healthy eating habits are important for good health.

Reviewing the Chapter

SCIENCE WORDS

A. Copy the sentences below. Use science terms from the chapter to complete the sentences.

1. The foods you eat are all part of your ___.
2. The parts of food that help your body grow and give you energy are called ___.
3. Two foods your body uses for quick energy are ___.
4. Foods stored in your body that can be used for extra energy are called ___.

B. Write the letter of the term that best matches the definition. Not all the terms will be used.

1. Food that contains starch
2. Nutrient that makes up over one half of your body
3. Food that contains sugar
4. Nutrients that help your body rebuild worn-out parts
5. Nutrients that are used for energy
6. Food that has fat in it.

a. apple
b. vitamins
c. nuts
d. diet
e. water
f. bread
g. minerals

UNDERSTANDING IDEAS

A. Identify each of the following.

1. I am a nutrient. I help your body to grow. I am found in meat, chicken, fish, eggs, and cheese. What am I?
2. I am a mineral. I am important for healthy blood. I am found in liver and green vegetables. What am I?

B. Make a chart like the one shown. Write the name of each food under the correct heading of the chart.

Meat group	Bread and cereal group	Fruit and vegetable group	Milk group

After completing the chart, tell which foods come from plants and which foods come from animals.

C. Name the six main kinds of nutrients.

USING IDEAS

1. Plan a menu for breakfast, lunch, and dinner. Include the right amount of food from each of the four food groups.

Science in Careers

Many people help to keep you healthy. You can name *doctors, dentists,* and *nurses.* But there are many other health workers.

Many people work for city health departments. Among other duties they make sure that health laws are obeyed.

Food inspectors check meat, fruits, and vegetables before they are sold. They make sure the food did not come from diseased animals or plants.

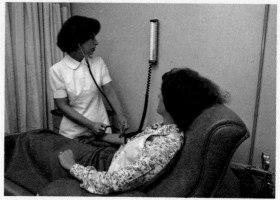
Nurse

Paramedics (par'ə med iks) work closely with doctors. They give emergency treatment to sick and injured people.

Pharmacists (fär'mə sists) make up the medicines ordered by doctors for sick people.

Dietitians (dī ə tish'ənz) plan meals needed for good health.

Food inspectors

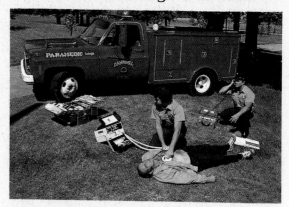
Paramedics

People in Science

Dr. Jane C. Wright (1919–)

Dr. Wright did not plan to be a doctor. Her goal was to become a famous artist. Today Dr. Wright teaches at the medical school where she was once a student. But her main interest is cancer research. She is trying to find a cure for cancer. She feels that someday cancer will be curable with drugs. Dr. Wright is trying to find those drugs.

Doctor doing cancer research

Developing Skills

WORD SKILLS

Prefixes and suffixes are word parts. A prefix is added to the beginning of a base word. A suffix is added to the end of a base word. The tables show how some prefixes and suffixes change the meanings of words.

Prefix	Meaning	Example
mis- re- un-	wrong again not	misplace reopen unhappy

Suffix	Meaning	Example
-er -less -y	more without like	warmer waterless milky

Use the tables to write meanings for these words.

1. cooler
2. mistrust
3. seedless
4. dusty
5. reheat
6. meatless
7. rewrap
8. unsafe

READING A BAR GRAPH

The graph on the next page is a bar graph. It shows the heights of students. The graph also shows how many students are the same height.

Use the graph to answer these questions.

1. The most students are what height?
2. The fewest students are what height?
3. How many students are 126 centimeters tall?
4. What is the difference in height between the tallest student and the shortest student?

HEIGHTS OF THIRD GRADERS

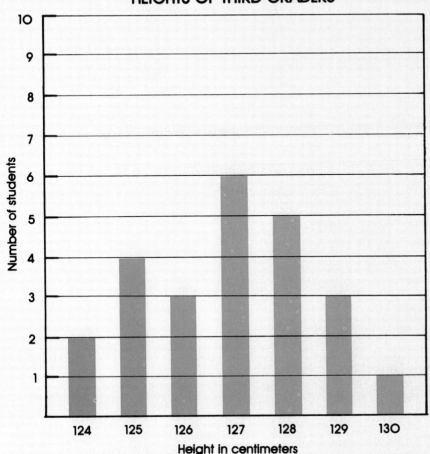

MAKING A BAR GRAPH

Make a bar graph to show how many times you eat foods from each of the four food groups. To gather your information, write the names of the four food groups in a list. Put a check next to the correct group each time you eat one of these foods. Do this for three or more days. Use this information to make your bar graph.

When the bar graph is completed, you will see if you are eating foods from each of the food groups.

Metric Measurement

In this book you will learn about measuring many different things. These things are measured in units of the metric system. To help you understand the metric system, look at the following drawings. Then look around your home and school for other things that are measured in metric units.

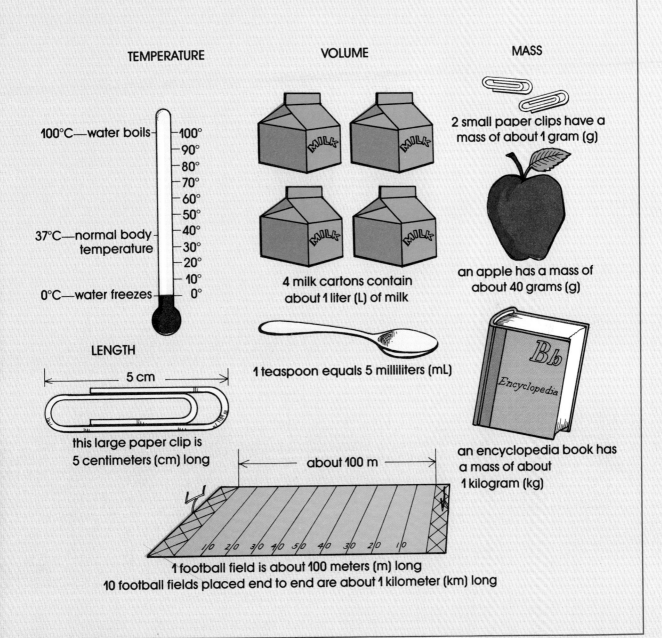

TEMPERATURE

100°C—water boils —100°
—90°
—80°
—70°
—60°
—50°
—40°
37°C—normal body—30°
temperature —20°
—10°
0°C—water freezes— 0°

LENGTH

5 cm

this large paper clip is
5 centimeters (cm) long

VOLUME

4 milk cartons contain
about 1 liter (L) of milk

1 teaspoon equals 5 milliliters (mL)

about 100 m

1/0 2/0 3/0 4/0 5/0 4/0 3/0 2/0 1/0

1 football field is about 100 meters (m) long
10 football fields placed end to end are about 1 kilometer (km) long

MASS

2 small paper clips have a
mass of about 1 gram (g)

an apple has a mass of
about 40 grams (g)

Bb

Encyclopedia

an encyclopedia book has
a mass of about
1 kilogram (kg)

Lesson Questions

To the student

Reading your book will help you learn more about the world around you. Your book will provide answers to many questions you may have about living things, the earth, space, matter, and energy.

On the following pages you will find questions from each lesson in your book. These questions will help test your understanding of the terms and ideas you read about.

There are two kinds of questions. You can answer the first kind by using the information you read in each lesson. Careful reading will help answer these questions.

The second type of question is called "Thinking like a Scientist." These questions are more challenging. The answer may not be found just by reading the lesson. You may have to think harder.

1 Animals

ANIMALS AND THEIR YOUNG

(pp. 4–7)

1. Where do most animals come from?
2. What are animals that are born alive and are given milk from the mother called?
3. How do some animals differ in the number of eggs they lay?
4. Name an animal that produces young hatched from eggs inside the mother's body.

Thinking like a Scientist

You are going to hatch a chicken egg, using a light bulb as a source of heat. You are told it is important to turn the egg every few hours. Why is doing this important?

ANIMALS GROW AND CHANGE

(pp. 8–12)

1. What are the three stages of growth of a grasshopper?

2. Name the stages of growth of the butterfly shown in the pictures.

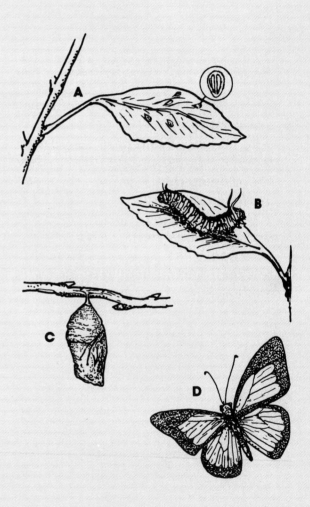

Thinking like a Scientist

Scientists learn about animals by carefully gathering information about them. How do scientists know that animals grow and change?

CARING FOR THE YOUNG

(pp. 13–17)

1. Write the name of each animal below. Then write *needs care when young* or *takes care of itself when young* for each.

   fish   kitten
   bird   turtle

2. Give three reasons why many newborn mammals need care.

Thinking like a Scientist

Most animals are born or hatched in the spring. Think of some reasons to explain this.

2 Animals Are Important

FOODS FROM ANIMALS

(pp. 22–24)

1. Which animals are called poultry?
2. Name the animal each food comes from.
   a. beef   b. bacon
   c. ham   d. milk
3. Name some animals used for food that are not raised by people.

Thinking like a Scientist

Sometimes a farmer's crop fails or a herd of animals becomes ill. How can science help farmers with problems like these?

PEOPLE RAISE OTHER ANIMALS

(pp. 25–28)

1. Tell how each animal is useful to people:
   a. dog
   b. horse

2. Explain what the item in each drawing is made of and name the animal it came from.

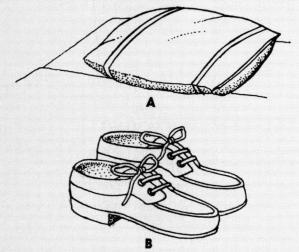

Thinking like a Scientist

You are lost in the wilderness. You are without food, warm clothing, and shelter. There are very few plants and they are all poisonous. You find three tame animals. One is large and covered with fur. The other two are small and covered with feathers. Write a short story telling how you would use these animals to survive.

ENDANGERED ANIMALS

(pp. 29–33)

1. What is blubber? How was it used?
2. What happened to whales after so many were hunted and killed?
3. Tell why each of these wild animals is endangered.

Thinking like a Scientist

Scientists can learn about pollution by observing and studying animals. What things would a scientist want to observe?

A

B

ANIMALS NEED PEOPLE

(pp. 34–35)

1. What is a wildlife refuge?
2. What is the difference between an endangered animal and an extinct animal?
3. Tell two ways wild animals are protected.

Thinking like a Scientist

Measuring and counting are very important learning tools that scientists use every day. Some scientists try to find out how many endangered animals of one kind exist in a large region. How could they find out the total number of endangered animals in a large region without counting each one?

3 Seed Plants

ROOTS
(pp. 40–42)
1. What do roots do for a plant?
2. Name the kinds of roots shown in the drawings. Tell how the roots are alike.

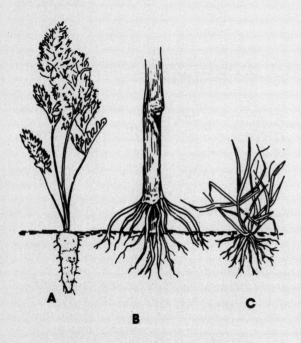

A B C

Thinking like a Scientist
Why might plants growing very close together be much smaller than normal?

STEMS
(pp. 43–47)
1. What do stems do for plants?
2. What are the four main kinds of seed plants?
3. Describe the stem of a tree.
4. How are the stems of herbs and vines different?

Thinking like a Scientist
Why are tomato plants often held up by wooden stakes?

LEAVES
(pp. 48–50)
1. Where do green plants make their food?
2. What food do leaves make?
3. Where do green plants get each of the following: water, energy, carbon dioxide?

Thinking like a Scientist

Pretend you are a scientist who is going to live on a strange planet. The planet has very little oxygen in the air. Instead the air is mostly carbon dioxide. Make a plan for putting more oxygen into the air.

FLOWERS AND SEEDS

(pp. 51–56)

1. How are all seeds alike?
2. Where do seeds come from?

3. Write the names of the seed parts shown in the drawing.

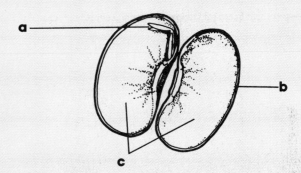

Thinking like a Scientist

How could you identify a strange seed? Describe three different things you could do.

297

4 Plants Are Important

FOOD FROM PLANTS

(pp. 62–69)

1. What is starch? How is it made?
2. What parts of these green plants are used as food?

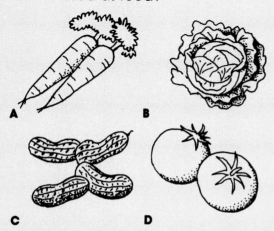

A
B
C
D

3. Why would there be no meat, milk, or eggs without green plants?

Thinking like a Scientist

Plan a dinner that includes all the parts of plants. You may use different kinds of plants in the meal.

OTHER USES OF PLANTS

(pp. 70–74)

1. What are these trees being used for?

2. What is compost?

Thinking like a Scientist

Some people do not live near a store that sells gardening supplies. How can these people get seeds, stakes, and fertilizer? How can they control insects?

HARMFUL PLANTS

(pp. 75–76)

1. How is mold harmful?
2. What is this plant? How is it helpful? How is it harmful?

3. Why are some plants not safe to eat or touch?

Thinking like a Scientist

Scientists who study plants know which ones are harmful. How do you think they learned which ones are not safe to eat?

5 All About Matter

PROPERTIES OF MATTER
(pp. 88–90)
1. Name some properties of objects.
2. What is matter?
3. What is mass?

Thinking like a Scientist
Scientists choose their words very carefully. Why are words like *mass, solid, liquid,* and *gas* important words to scientists?

STATES OF MATTER
(pp. 91–93)
1. How many states of matter are there? Name them.
2. List each state of matter and give an example.

Thinking like a Scientist
Try to predict what would happen if liquid was not a state of matter on the earth.

THE PARTICLES IN MATTER
(pp. 94–95)
1. Draw three squares. Label the squares *A, B,* and *C.* Draw particles in the squares as they might look in each of these things.

A   B   C

Thinking like a Scientist
When water gets very cold, it freezes into a solid. Solid ice floats on water. Why is it important to some fish that ice is lighter than water? Draw two squares. Label one square *water* and the other *ice.* Draw particles of water in one square and particles of ice in the other.

MATTER CAN CHANGE

(pp. 96–98)

1. What is a physical change?
2. Tell what happens to water at each temperature.

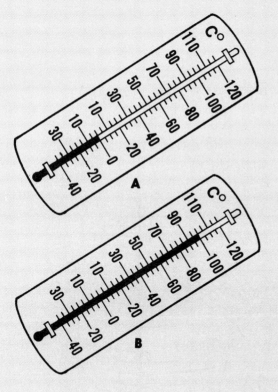

Thinking like a Scientist

How can changing states of water be a problem for people?

DIFFERENT KINDS OF MATTER

(pp. 99–101)

1. How is a chemical change very different from a physical change?
2. Give an example of a chemical change.
3. Tell how matter becomes different in a chemical change.

Thinking like a Scientist

The following are chemical changes. What is needed to make each change take place?

1. wood to ashes
2. flour, water, yeast to bread
3. baking soda to carbon dioxide
4. iron to rust

6   *Force, Work, and Energy*

FORCES
(pp. 106–108)
1. What is a force?
2. Name at least three ways in which forces change the motion of things.
3. Give an example of a pushing force and a pulling force.

Thinking like a Scientist
Are forces a form of matter? Why or why not?

KINDS OF FORCES
(pp. 109–114)
1. What is gravity?
2. Describe the kind of force that is acting between each pair of magnets as a push or a pull.

A | S   N | N   S |

B | S   N | S   N |

C | N   S | S   N |

3. What is friction?
4. How can friction be reduced?

Thinking like a Scientist
Reducing friction on spacecraft can be a problem for scientists. In space, lubricants evaporate because of the heat from the sun. Why would this evaporation be a problem?

WORK
(pp. 115–116)
1. When is work done?
2. Which pictures show no work being done?

A

B

C

Thinking like a Scientist

Which is more work—pushing a shopping cart 2 meters or pushing a shopping cart 8 meters? Explain your answer.

ENERGY
(pp. 117–119)

1. How are energy and work related?
2. The terms below are out of order. Write the terms in the correct order.

Something moves   Energy is
                    needed

Work is done   Force is used

3. The amount of work that is done depends on two things. What are they?

Thinking like a Scientist

There are many kinds of energy. Can energy change from one kind to another? If so, give three examples of energy that changes from one kind to another. If not, explain why not.

7 *Machines*

THE LEVER—A SIMPLE MACHINE

(pp. 124–127)

1. What is a simple machine?
2. Name five ways machines are used at your school.
3. Identify the force, the load, and the turning point in the picture.

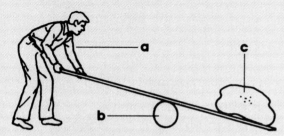

Thinking like a Scientist

Look at the lever below. How can you change the lever to reduce the force needed to lift the load? How could you change the lever so that you push down less distance to move the load a greater distance?

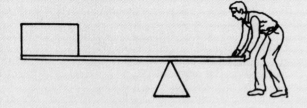

USING AN INCLINED PLANE

(pp. 128–131)

1. What is an inclined plane?
2. How do the force and the load move when an inclined plane is used?
3. What is a wedge?
4. What kind of machine is a screw?

Thinking like a Scientist

What simple machines might be used on a camping trip? Give as many examples as you can.

THE WHEEL AND AXLE

(pp. 132–134)

1. Give an example of a wheel and axle. How does it make work easier?
2. What is a gear?

Thinking like a Scientist

Look at the gears. How many times would gear A go around for each turn of gear B? Explain how this could be useful in a machine.

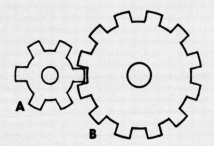

PULLEYS
(pp. 135–137)

1. What is a pulley?
2. What simple machine is shown in the picture? Describe how the force and load move.

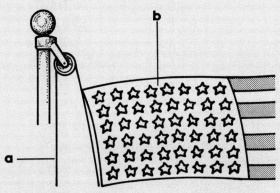

3. Identify the force and the load in the picture. Explain how the pulley is being used to make it easier to do work.

Thinking like a Scientist
You have been given a job. You must get a bucket of sand to the third floor of a building. You cannot use the stairs or the elevator to get the bucket there. There is an open window on the third floor. Tell or use a drawing to show how you would get the bucket to the third floor.

COMPOUND MACHINES
(pp. 138–139)

1. What are compound machines?
2. Identify three objects that are compound machines.

Thinking like a Scientist
Look at the compound machine. Name the simple machines that are part of the compound machine and tell how each helps to do work.

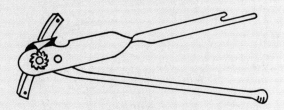

8 Sound

MAKING SOUND
(pp. 144–145)
1. How is sound made?
2. How is a vibrating drum like a vibrating ruler?

Thinking like a Scientist
Sometimes breakfast cereals make popping sounds in milk. A popping balloon makes a similar sound. What do you think causes these popping sounds?

DIFFERENT SOUNDS
(pp. 146–148)
1. What is the difference between the volume and pitch of sounds?
2. List these instruments by pitch (1 = highest and 4 = lowest).

Thinking like a Scientist
Why would a guitar player keep tightening the strings on the guitar? Why do pianos need tuning?

HOW SOUND MOVES
(pp. 149–151)
1. Through which kind of matter does sound move fastest?
2. How can you use sound to tell if a train is coming from far away?

Thinking like a Scientist
Design an experiment to prove that sound moves better through some things than it does through others.

HOW SOUND BOUNCES
(pp. 152–153)
1. What is a reflected sound?
2. When can an echo be heard?

Thinking like a Scientist

Why are auditoriums designed like this?

SOUNDS MADE BY LIVING THINGS

(pp. 154–157)

1. What is communication?
2. What are vocal cords?
3. How do bats use sounds to locate objects?

Thinking like a Scientist

Underwater submarines can find other objects in the water. How do you think they are able to do this?

9 *The Changing Earth*

INSIDE THE EARTH
(pp. 168–170)

1. Look at the drawing. Name the three layers of the earth.

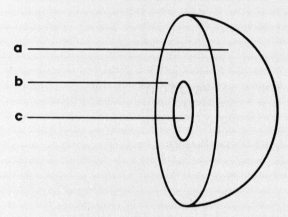

2. Give two reasons why the crust is the most important layer of the earth.

Thinking like a Scientist

You are given a hot roll to eat. It is too hot to bite into. After you wait a few minutes, the outside becomes cooler and harder. You bite into the roll. It is still so hot that steam comes from the middle. Explain your finding. How is the roll like the earth?

FAST CHANGES IN THE CRUST
(pp. 171–173)

1. How does an earthquake cause a change in the crust?
2. What is a volcano?

Thinking like a Scientist

Scientists are trying to predict exactly when earthquakes will occur. What science facts might be important in predicting earthquakes? Why? Why is this type of scientific work important?

SLOWER CHANGES IN THE CRUST
(pp. 174–175)

1. What is weathering?
2. What is erosion?

Thinking like a Scientist

Tell two ways that you could stop erosion on a steep hillside.

CHANGES CAUSED BY WATER
(pp. 176–178)

1. What causes rocks in and near a river to become round and smooth?
2. How does freezing water weather rocks?

Thinking like a Scientist
Explain why many roads are in poor condition after a hard winter.

CHANGES CAUSED BY WIND
(pp. 179–180)

1. How can strong winds change the earth's crust?
2. How does moving sand weather rock?

Thinking like a Scientist
You live next to a desert. Winds constantly blow sand into your house. Make a plan to prevent this from happening.

CHANGES CAUSED BY LIVING THINGS
(pp. 181–183)

1. Explain how this living thing is changing the earth's crust.

2. What is one way that people change the earth's crust?

Thinking like a Scientist
Many workers make their living by digging into the earth's crust. Name three jobs that depend on the earth's crust.

10 The Earth's Resources

SOIL AS A RESOURCE

(pp. 188–190)

1. What are natural resources?
2. What is soil made of?
3. What is humus?

Thinking like a Scientist

Tell why you would not find much humus in a desert. Where would you expect to find the most humus?

THE AIR AROUND US

(pp. 191–194)

1. What is wind?
2. Which gas makes up most of the air?
3. What is the air around the earth called?
4. How do each of the following cause pollution: wind, volcanoes, factories, cars?

Thinking like a Scientist

Scientists often use models to help explain their ideas. The models make the ideas easier to understand. They can also help describe things. How is an orange rind on an orange like the earth and its atmosphere?

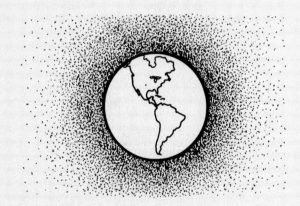

THE EARTH'S WATER SUPPLY

(pp. 195–197)

1. What is a reservoir?
2. Describe irrigation.
3. Name four places where water may be found.

Thinking like a Scientist

Describe four ways people can use water from a reservoir.

ENERGY FROM THE EARTH

(pp. 198–199)

1. Name three fuels that come from the earth's crust.
2. Why are fuels important natural resources?
3. When do fuels give off energy?

Thinking like a Scientist

Why is it so important not to waste natural resources such as coal, oil, and gas?

SOME OTHER RESOURCES

(pp. 200–201)

1. What are ores?
2. Why are metals important natural resources?

3. What are gems?
4. How are these natural resources used?

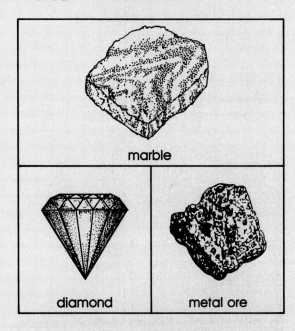

marble

diamond

metal ore

Thinking like a Scientist

Make a list of how metals are used in your home. How would your life be different without these metals?

11 The Weather Around You

HEATING THE EARTH
(pp. 206–207)

1. What happens to sunlight as it strikes the earth?
2. Why is it warmer on a sunny day than on a cloudy day?

Thinking like a Scientist

Suppose two cities had the same temperature one day. They also had the same amount of water in the air. One city had clouds covering it at night and one did not. Which city would have a cooler night? Why?

SEASONS
(pp. 208–210)

1. Why is it warmer in summer than in winter?
2. What causes the seasons?

Thinking like a Scientist

It always seems very cold around the North Pole and the South Pole. Tell why these areas are so cold.

HEATING DIFFERENT SURFACES
(pp. 211–212)

1. Why is air over water cooler than air over land during the day?
2. Which box would absorb the most light? Why?

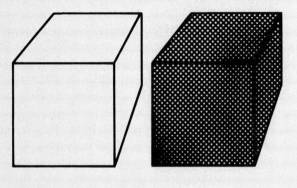

A   B

3. Explain how differences in temperature cause air to move.

Thinking like a Scientist

In cold places, bridges often have a sign that reads: "Bridge freezes before roadway." Why do you think water on a bridge freezes first?

WATER IN THE AIR

(pp. 213–214)

1. What happens to water in a puddle when the sun shines?
2. What is dew?

Thinking like a Scientist

Astronauts sometimes have a problem with water in the air. They have a machine like a vacuum cleaner to help them take showers aboard the Space Shuttle. What do you think this machine does?

CLOUDS

(pp. 215–217)

1. Tell where in the sky each of the clouds shown forms.

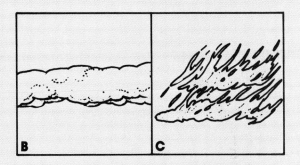

2. Which clouds often bring rain?

Thinking like a Scientist

On some days it is cloudy but it does not rain. On other days it is cloudy and it rains. Explain why this happens.

WATER CYCLE

(pp. 218–220)

1. What are the three things that could happen to rain after it falls?
2. What is a water cycle?

Thinking like a Scientist

What would happen to the water cycle if oil covered the oceans?

12 Sun, Moon, and Planets

LOOKING AT THE MOON AND THE SUN
(pp. 226–229)
1. Why does the moon appear larger than any of the stars in the sky?
2. Write the names of the areas of the moon shown in the picture.

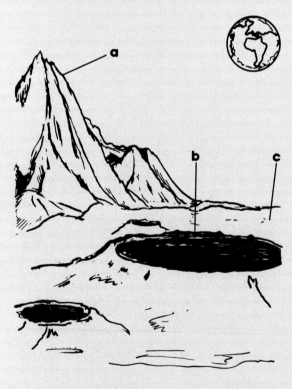

3. What is the sun made of?

Thinking like a Scientist
Sometimes scientists can figure out answers to questions without observing. Scientists are pretty sure how craters on the moon were formed. They have never watched one form. They have seen many craterlike shapes formed on the earth. How could you use a rock and mud to demonstrate how a crater forms?

MOTIONS IN SPACE
(pp. 230–231)
1. Why is the moon called a satellite?
2. What is an orbit?
3. What is the difference between a rotation and a revolution?

Thinking like a Scientist
The earth revolves and rotates. Many things around you revolve and rotate. Name three things that revolve and three that rotate.

PHASES OF THE MOON

(pp. 232–233)

1. How long does it take the moon to make one orbit around the earth?
2. During which half of the moon's orbit can more and more of the moon be seen each night?

Thinking like a Scientist

One half of the lighted side of the moon can be seen during first and last quarter. Explain how the moon is different in these two quarters.

ECLIPSES

(pp. 234–236)

1. Write the kind of eclipse shown in each drawing.

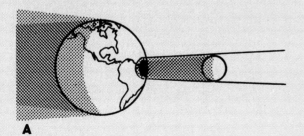

A

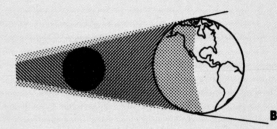

B

Thinking like a Scientist

Eclipses of the moon and sun were often frightening to people who lived long ago. Why do you suppose they were afraid?

THE PLANETS

(pp. 237–239)

1. How many known planets are there?
2. What large objects make up the solar system?
3. Which planets are hotter than the earth? Why?

Thinking like a Scientist

In 1979, Pluto became closer to the sun than Neptune. Pluto will be closer than Neptune for the next 20 years. In what ways will these two planets be different for the next 20 years?

13 Good Health Habits

KEEPING YOURSELF CLEAN

(pp. 250–253)

1. What are habits?
2. Tell what good health habit is being practiced in each picture.

A

B

C

Thinking like a Scientist

Inventors often help solve scient problems. Name five inventions th make good health habits at home easier.

TEETH CARE

(pp. 254–256)

1. When is it best to brush your tee
2. What is plaque?
3. What causes teeth to decay?
4. Why should you visit a dentist?

Thinking like a Scientist

Pretend you are doing a study on tooth decay. Group A eats mostly fresh meats, vegetables, and fruit. Group B eats a large amount of candy, cakes, and soft drinks. After 1 year, group B has many more cavities than group A. What conclusion would you make?

EXERCISE AND SLEEP

(pp. 257–260)

1. Why is exercise important to your health?
2. How often should you exercise?
3. Why does your body need sleep?

Thinking like a Scientist

Make up an experiment to prove that sleep is important.

SAFETY HABITS

(pp. 261–263)

1. Give three safety habits for riding bicycles.

2. Tell when the hand signal in each drawing should be used.

Thinking like a Scientist

Scientists do experiments to learn how people see colors. These show that lighter colors are seen more easily at night than darker ones. How have people used this fact in teaching safety habits?

14 Nutrition

THE NEED FOR FOOD

(pp. 268–269)

1. Why is the food you eat important to your body?
2. Name three foods that have a lot of energy.

Thinking like a Scientist

Long-distance runners eat a lot of bread, potatoes, and spaghetti-type foods on the days before a race. Why do you think they do this?

KINDS OF FOOD

(pp. 270–274)

1. What are nutrients?
2. Write the name of a nutrient found in each of these things.

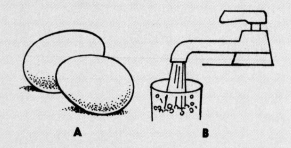

Thinking like a Scientist

Long ago, sailors often had a skin disease called scurvy. While sailing, they did not eat oranges and other fruits and vegetables. Fruits and vegetables did not stay fresh on the ship. On shore the sailors did eat fruits and vegetables. They did not get scurvy on shore very often. Describe what you think was happening to the sailors' bodies.

FOOD GROUPS

(pp. 275–278)

1. What is a balanced diet?
2. Look at the table below. Find the mistakes. Write the correct group each food comes from.

milk products	meat
eggs	butter
bread	nuts
pears	cheese

fruits and vegetables	breads and cereals
milk	rice
onions	fish
pork	peas

Thinking like a Scientist

Astronauts need a balanced diet. Space scientists did tests to learn what foods were easy to carry aboard a spacecraft. Predict what food groups were difficult to cook, eat, and store in space.

HEALTHY EATING HABITS

(pp. 279–281)

1. Name two healthy eating habits.
2. What happens if you eat more food than your body needs?
3. Why should you eat natural foods?

Thinking like a Scientist

Pretend you are a doctor. You have a patient who is dangerously overweight. Describe three different plans for your patient to slowly lose weight.

GLOSSARY

Key to Pronunciation

a apple, bat	**i** if, pig	**sh** she, wish	**ə** stands for:
ā ate, page	**ī** idea, fine	**th** think, moth	a in asleep
â air, care	**ng** ring, sink	**ŦH** the, bathe	e in garden
ä father, star	**o** ox, top	**u** uncle, sun	i in pencil
ch chest, such	**ō** owe, no	**ù** pull, foot	o in button
e egg, bed	**ô** orbit, saw	**ü** glue, boot	u in circus
ē even, me	**oi** oil, joy	**zh** usual, vision	
ėr earn, bird	**ou** out, mouse		

This Key to Pronunciation is adapted from *Scott, Foresman Intermediate Dictionary*, by E. L. Thorndike and Clarence L. Barnhart. Copyright © 1983 by Scott, Foresman and Company. Reprinted by permission.

adult   The final stage in the growth of animals. *p. 10*

atmosphere (at′mə sfir)   The layer of air that surrounds the earth. *p. 193*

atom (at′əm)   The smallest particle that makes up matter. *p. 94*

balance (bal′əns)   A tool used to measure mass. *p. 89*

boiling point   The temperature at which water begins to boil (100°C). *p. 97*

carbon dioxide (kär′bən dī ok′sīd)   A gas found in the air. Plants use carbon dioxide to make food. *p. 48*

cavity (kav′ə tē)   A hole in the outside covering of a tooth that is caused by decay. *p. 255*

chemical change   When one kind of matter becomes a different kind of matter. *p. 99*

cloud   Millions of tiny water drops that form when water vapor collects on bits of dust. *p. 215*

communication (kə myü nə kā′shən)   The sending of messages. *p. 154*

compost (kom′pōst)   A mixture made of rotted plant materials. Compost is used to restore minerals to the soil. *p. 71*

compound machine   A machine that is made of two or more simple machines. *p. 138*

condensation (kon den sā′shən)   The change from a gas to a liquid. *p. 98*

core (kôr)   The layer of the earth under the mantle. The core is the hottest part of the earth. *p. 169*

320

crater (krā′tər)   A bowl-shaped area found on the surface of the moon. *p. 228*

crust (krust)   The outer layer of the earth. The crust is mostly solid rock. *p. 168*

dental floss (flôs)   A special kind of thread that is used to clean teeth. *p. 255*

dew   Drops of water that form when water vapor in the air touches cool objects. *p. 214*

diet (dī′ət)   All the food you eat. *p. 275*

down   Soft feathers from birds such as ducks and geese. *p. 25*

earthquake (ėrth′kwāk)   A movement of the layers of rock in the earth's crust. *p. 171*

echo (ek′ō)   A sound that bounces back after it hits an object. *p. 153*

eclipse (i klips′)   The effect produced when one body in space passes into the shadow of another body in space. *p. 234*

eclipse of the moon   A darkening of the moon as it passes into the earth's shadow. *p. 235*

eclipse of the sun   A darkening of the sun as the moon passes between the sun and the earth. *p. 235*

egg   The first stage of growth of some kinds of animals. The egg contains everything needed to form a new animal. *p. 9*

endangered (en dān′jərd)   When only a few of a certain kind of plant or animal remain. *p. 29*

energy   The ability to do work. *p. 117*

erosion (i rō′zhən)   The movement of rock, sand, or soil by water or wind. *p. 175*

evaporation (i vap ə rā′shən)   The change from a liquid to a gas. *p. 98*

extinct (ek stingkt′)   When a kind of plant or animal is gone forever. *p. 34*

fat   One of the six main kinds of nutrients your body needs. *p. 271*

fibrous (fī′brəs) **root**   One of many small roots. Fibrous roots are all about the same size. *p. 41*

fixed pulley   A pulley that stays in one place when it is being used. *p. 136*

force (fôrs)   A push or a pull that is needed to make something move. *p. 106*

freezing point   The temperature at which water begins to freeze (0°C). *p. 97*

friction (frik'shən)   A kind of force that slows down or stops motion. *p. 113*

frost   Ice crystals that form when water vapor freezes on objects. *p. 214*

fuel   A material that can be broken down to release energy. *p. 198*

gas   A state of matter. A gas always has the same shape as the container it fills. *p. 91*

gear   A kind of simple machine that is like a wheel and axle. A gear is a wheel with teeth. *p. 134*

gem (jem)   A beautiful mineral, such as a diamond, that is sometimes found in a rock. *p. 201*

germ (jėrm)   A tiny living thing that can make people sick. *p. 250*

germinate (jėr'mə nāt)   To grow from a seed into a new plant. *p. 55*

grain (grān)   A seed from certain grasses, such as oats, wheat, rice, and corn. *p. 65*

gravity (grav'ə tē)   The force of one object pulling on another object. Gravity pulls things toward the earth. *p. 109*

habit (hab'it)   Something that can be done without thinking. *p. 250*

herb (ėrb)   A kind of seed plant that is small and has a soft stem. *p. 46*

hide   The skin of animals such as cattle, sheep, and pigs. *p. 26*

humus (hyü'məs)   Bits of plant and animal matter found in soil. Humus returns useful materials to the soil. *p. 189*

inclined (in klīnd') **plane**   A kind of simple machine. An inclined plane is a slanted surface that makes it easier to move an object to a higher place. *p. 128*

irrigation (ir ə gā'shən)   The watering of crops when there is not enough rain. *p. 196*

larva (lär'və)   The second stage of growth of some kinds of insects. *p. 9*

lava (lä'və)   Melted rock that flows from a volcano. *p. 173*

lever (lev'ər)   A kind of simple machine used to lift or move things. *p. 125*

liquid (lik'wid)   A state of matter. A liquid always has the same shape as its container. *p. 91*

load   The object to be lifted or moved by a machine. *p. 125*

lubricant (lü'brə kənt)   A substance, such as oil or grease, that reduces friction. *p. 114*

machine   Any tool that can help people to do work. *p. 124*

magma (mag′mə) Melted rock that is inside the earth's crust. *p. 172*

magnetism (mag′nə tiz əm) A force that acts on some kinds of metals. *p. 112*

mammal (mam′əl) An animal that has hair and feeds its young with mother's milk. *p. 6*

mantle (man′təl) The layer of the earth that lies beneath the crust. The mantle is made of rocklike material. *p. 169*

mass The measure of how much matter there is in an object. *p. 89*

matter Anything that takes up space and has mass. *p. 88*

mildew (mil′dü) A kind of nongreen plant that grows in shady, damp places. *p. 75*

minerals One of the six main kinds of nutrients your body needs. *p. 272*

movable pulley A pulley that moves as a load is moved. *p. 136*

natural resources (nach′ər əl ri sôr′siz) Useful materials that come from the earth. *p. 188*

nutrient (nü′trē ənts) The part of food that helps a person grow and gives energy. *p. 270*

nymph (nimf) The second stage of growth of some kinds of insects. A nymph is like a tiny adult without wings. *p. 11*

orbit (ôr′bit) The path a satellite follows. *p. 230*

ore (ôr) A rock that contains metal. *p. 200*

oxygen (ok′sə jən) A gas found in the air. Plants give off oxygen. Most living things need oxygen to stay alive. *p. 49*

phase (fāz) A change in the way the moon looks when it is seen from the earth. *p. 232*

physical (fiz′ə kəl) **change** Any change in the size, shape, or state of matter. *p. 96*

pitch The highness or lowness of sound. *p. 147*

planet (plan′it) A body that revolves around the sun. There are nine planets in the solar system. *p. 237*

plaque (plak) A sticky film that forms on the surfaces of teeth. Plaque can cause teeth to decay. *p. 255*

pollution (pə lü′shən) Anything dirty in the earth's water or air. *p. 193*

poultry (pōl'trē)   Birds such as chickens and turkeys that are used for food. *p. 23*

precipitation (pri sip ə tā'shen) Water that falls in the form of rain, hail, snow, or sleet. *p. 217*

prop roots   Extra roots that grow out from the sides of stems. *p. 42*

protein (prō'tēn)   One of the six main kinds of nutrients your body needs. *p. 271*

pulley (pül'ē)   A kind of simple machine. A pulley is a wheel with a rope around it. It is used to move objects to places that are hard to reach. *p. 135*

pupa (pyü'pə)   The third stage of growth of some kinds of insects. A pupa lives inside a hard covering. *p. 9*

reflected sound   A sound that has changed the direction of its movement. *p. 152*

reservoir (rez'ər vwär)   A place where water is stored. *p. 196*

revolution (rev ə lü'shən)   The motion of the earth and the moon in their orbits. *p. 231*

rotation (rō tā'shən)   The spinning motion of some bodies in space. *p. 231*

satellite (sat'ə līt)   A body in space that moves around a larger body. *p. 230*

screw   A kind of simple machine that is like an inclined plane wrapped around a center post. *p. 130*

seed coat   A seed covering. *p. 54*

shrub   A kind of seed plant that is smaller than a tree and has many woody stems. *p. 45*

simple machine   A machine with few or no moving parts. *p. 124*

sleet   Frozen drops of rain. *p. 217*

snowflakes   Ice crystals that form from water vapor when the temperature in a cloud is below freezing. *p. 217*

solar system (sō'lər sis'təm)   The sun and the planets that revolve around it. *p. 237*

solid   A state of matter. A solid always has a shape of its own. *p. 91*

starch (stärch)   Food stored in the seeds, roots, stems, and leaves of green plants. *p. 62*   One of the six main kinds of nutrients your body needs. *p. 270*

sugar   One of the six main kinds of nutrients your body needs. *p. 270*

sun flare A giant stream of glowing gas that explodes from the surface of the sun. *p. 229*

taproot A large main root. *p. 41*

topsoil The top layer of soil. *p. 189*

tree A kind of seed plant that has one main stem called a trunk. *p. 45*

vibration (vī brā′shən) The back-and-forth movement of matter. Some vibrations cause sound. *p. 144*

vine A kind of seed plant that has soft stems and climbs as it grows. *p. 47*

vitamins (vī′tə mins) One of the six main kinds of nutrients your body needs. *p. 272*

vocal (vō′kəl) **cords** Special flaps of muscle found in the throat. They move back and forth to make sounds in the throat. *p. 154*

volcano (vol kā′nō) An opening in the earth's crust through which hot melted rock flows. *p. 172*

volume (vol′yəm) The loudness or softness of sound. *p. 146*

water One of the six main kinds of nutrients your body needs. *p. 273*

water cycle (sī′kəl) The change in the state of water that happens over and over again. *p. 218*

water vapor (vā′pər) Water in the form of a gas. *p. 96*

weathering (weŦH′ər ing) The wearing away and breaking of rock by moving water and wind. *p. 174*

wedge (wej) A kind of simple machine formed by two inclined planes. *p. 129*

wheel and axle (ak′səl) A kind of simple machine that is made of a wheel that turns on a center post. *p. 132*

wildlife refuge (wīld′līf ref′yüj) A safe place were wild animals live. *p. 34*

wind The movement of air. *p. 212*

work The use of a force to move something. *p. 115*

INDEX

CREDITS

Cover: Taylor Oughton
Other art: Michael Adams, David Hanum, Kathy Hendricksen, Gregory Hergert, Phillip Jones, Joseph LeMonnier, John Lind, Rebecca Merrilees, Taylor Oughton, Heidi Palmer.

Unit One 1: *t.l.* E.R. Degginger; *m.l.* Tom Stack/Tom Stack & Associates; *b.l.* Leonard Lee Rue III; *t.m.* Grant Heilman Photography; *t.r.* Bob & Clara Calhoun/Bruce Coleman; *b.m.* Charles Paler—Earth Scenes/Animals Animals; *b.r.* Breck P. Kent.

Chapter 1 2–3: Carol Hughes/Bruce Coleman. 4: E.R. Degginger. 5: © Tom McHugh/Photo Researchers, Inc.; except *t.r.* Jane Burton/Bruce Coleman. 6: *t.l.* © Phil A. Dotson/Photo Researchers, Inc.; *b.l., b.r.* John Colwell/Grant Heilman Photography. 7: Victoria Beller-Smith for Silver Burdett. 8: Oxford Scientific Films/Animals Animals; except *b.r.* Sal Giordano III. 9: *l.* © James Dickinson/Photo Researchers, Inc.; *t.r.* Jen and Des Bartlett/Bruce Coleman; *b.r.* Grant Heilman Photography. 10: Grant Heilman Photography. 11: D.R. Specker/Animals Animals. 12: Victoria Beller-Smith for Silver Burdett. 13: Jen and Des Bartlett/Bruce Coleman. 14: *t.* © Arthur C. Twomey/Photo Researchers, Inc.; *b.* Arthus-Bertrand/Peter Arnold, Inc. 15: *t.l.* John Colwell/Grant Heilman Photography; *t.r.* Animals Animals; *b.l.* © Tom McHugh/Photo Researchers, Inc. 16: Stouffer Productions, Ltd./Animals Animals 17: C. Haagner/Bruce Coleman.

Chapter 2 20–21: Jen and Des Bartlett/Bruce Coleman. 22: *t.l.* Grant Heilman Photography; *b.l.* Dan De Wilde for Silver Burdett; *r.* Phil Degginger/Bruce Coleman. 23: *l.* Ronny Jaques/Photo Researchers, Inc.; *r.* Ted Spiegel/Black Star. 24: *t.r.* Bill Gillette/Stock, Boston; *b.* © Milton J. Heiberg/Photo Researchers, Inc. 25: Phil Degginger; *b.l.* Gerhard Gscheidle/Peter Arnold, Inc.; *r.* Silver Burdett. 26: Silver Burdett. 27: *t.* © E. Hanumantha/Photo Researchers, Inc.; *m.* Joe Monroe/Photo Researchers, Inc.; *b.* E.R. Degginger. 28: *t.* Silver Burdett. Dan De Wilde for Silver Burdett. 30: *t.* E.R. Degginger; *m.* © Kenneth W. Fink/National Audubon Society Collection/Photo Researchers, Inc.; *b.* Joe Van Wormer/Bruce Coleman. 31: *t.* © George Holton/Photo Researchers, Inc.; *b.* © Suen-O Lindblad/Photo Researchers, Inc.. 32: Jeff Foott/Bruce Coleman; *inset* David deVries/Bruce Coleman. 33: Victoria Beller-Smith for Silver Burdett. 34: *t.* Courtesy The American Museum of Natural History; *b.* Adolf Schmidecker/Alpha. 35: *l.* Jeff Foott/Bruce Coleman; *r.* Robert P. Carr/Bruce Coleman.

Chapter 3 38–40: E.R. Degginger. 42: Stephen J. Krasemann/Peter Arnold, Inc. 43: *t.* Runk/Schoenberger/Grant Heilman Photography; *b.l.* Dan Clark/Grant Heilman Photography; *b.r.* Grant Heilman Photography. 44:Silver Burdett. 45: © Kenneth W. Fink/Photo Researchers, Inc.; *b.l.* Leonard Lee Rue III; *b.r.* E.R. Degginger—Earth Scenes/Animals Animals. 46: *t.l.* © V.P. Weinland/Photo Researchers, Inc.; *t.r.* Rod Planck/Tom Stack & Associates; *b.r.* Grant Heilman Photography. 47: *t.l.* Grant Heilman Photography; *t.r.* Runk/Schoenberger/Grant Heilman Photography; *b.* E.R. Degginger. 49: *t.l.* © Tom McHugh/Photo Researchers, Inc.; *t.r.* Brian Milne—Earth Scenes/Animals Animals; *b.l.* Breck P. Kent. 50: Dan De Wilde for Silver Burdett. 51: *t.l.* E.R. Degginger; *t.r.* Holt Confer/Grant Heilman Photography; *m.r.* M. Austerman—Earth Scenes/Animals Animals; *b.l.* E.R. Degginger; *b.r.* Grant Heilman Photography. 52: *t.* W.H. Hodge/Peter Arnold, Inc; *all insets* Runk/Schoenberger/Grant Heilman Photography; *b.* John Colwell/Grant Heilman Photography. 53: *t.* Silver Burdett; *b.l., b.r.* Runk/Schoenberger/Grant Heilman Photography. 54: *t.* Silver Burdett; *r.* Breck P. Kent; *b.l.* Grant Heilman Photography. 55: © William Harlow/National Audubon Society/Photo Researchers, Inc. 56: Victoria Beller-Smith for Silver Burdett.

Chapter 4 60–61: Dan De Wilde for Silver Burdett. 62–64: Silver Burdett. 65: Grant Heilman Photography. 66: *l.* George Harrison/Bruce Coleman; *b.l.* Bruce Coleman; *r.* © Townsend P. Dickinson/Photo Researchers, Inc.; *inset* Barry L. Runk/Grant Heilman Photography. 67: Silver Burdett. 68: *t.* Silver Burdett; *b.* © 1985 John Blaustein/Woodfin Camp & Associates. 69: Silver Burdett. 70: *t.* Michael Newler/The Stock Shop; *b.* S. Rannels/Grant Heilman Photography. 71: *l., t.r.* Grant Heilman Photography; *b.r.* Robert P. Carr/Bruce Coleman. 72: *t.* Martin Rotker/Taurus Photos; *b.* © Dr. William Harlow/Photo Researchers, Inc. 73: *t.* Grant Heilman Photography; *m.* © Bruce Roberts/Photo Researchers, Inc.; *b.* Silver Burdett. 74: *t.l., m.l.* Silver Burdett; *b.l.* © Brian Brake/Photo Researchers, Inc.; *r.* Vance Henry/Taurus Photos; *inset* Hickson-Bender Photography for Silver Burdett. 75: *t.* D. Lyons/Bruce Coleman; *b.* © Russ Kinne/Photo Researchers, Inc. 77: Silver Burdett. 80: *l.* Kent and Donna Dannen/Photo Researchers, Inc.; *t.r.* © Charles R. Belinky/Photo Researchers, Inc.; *b.r.* © Larry Mulvehill/Photo Researchers, Inc. 81: Leonard Lee Rue III/Bruce Coleman.

Unit Two 84–85: *t.l.* Jim Tuten/Black Star; *b.l.* R.L. Williams/Taurus Photos; *t.r.* Focus on Sports; *b.r.* Dennis Hallinan/Freelance Photographers Guild.

Chapter 5 86–87: Silver Burdett. 88: Dan De Wilde for Silver Burdett. 89–95: Silver Burdett. 96: *l.* Silver Burdett; *r.* Dan De Wilde for Silver Burdett. 97: *l.* Issac Geib/Grant Heilman Photography; *r.* Larry P. Harris/Tom Stack & Associates. 98–99: Silver Burdett. 100: Victoria Beller-Smith for Silver Burdett. 101: Silver Burdett.

Chapter 6 104–105: Eric Carle/Shostal Associates. 106: *l.* Dan De Wilde for Silver Burdett; *r.* Imagery. 107: Silver Burdett. 108: Zimmerman/Alpha. 109: Ken Regan/Camera 5. 110: *t.* Courtesy, Los Angeles Dodgers; *b.* Dan De Wilde for Silver Burdett. 111–112: Silver Burdett. 113: Atoz Images. 114: Silver Burdett. 115: Richard Choy/Peter Arnold, Inc. 116: Silver Burdett. 117: *l.* Silver Burdett; *r.* David Lee Guss/Shostal Associates. 118: Dan De Wilde for Silver Burdett. 119: *t.* Bill Anderson/Shostal Associates; *b.* Eric Carle/Shostal Associates.

Chapter 7 122–123: Michal Heron. 124: *t.l., m.l.* Silver Burdett; *b.l.* Michael Philip Manheim/The Stock Shop; *b.r.* D.C. Lowe/Shostal Associates. 125: Dan De Wilde for Silver Burdett. 126: *t.l., t.r.* Dan De Wilde for Silver Burdett; *m.l., b.l.* Silver Burdett. 127–128: Silver Burdett. 129: *t.l.* Tom Myers; *t.r.* Silver Burdett; *b.r.* Michal Heron. 130–136: Silver Burdett. 137: Peter Beck/Alpha. 138–139: Silver Burdett.

Chapter 8 142–143: E.R. Degginger. 144–145: Silver Burdett. 146: Victoria Beller-Smith for Silver Burdett. 147: *l.* © Jim Carter/Photo Researchers, Inc.; *t.r.* © Gerry Souter/Photo Researchers, Inc.; *b.r.* E.R. Degginger. 148: Dan De Wilde for Silver Burdett. 149: NASA. 150: © Tom McHugh/Photo Researchers, Inc. 151: Silver Burdett. 152: Dan De Wilde for Silver Burdett. 153: *t.l., b.l.* Silver Burdett; *t.r., b.r.* Frank Siteman/Stock Boston. 155: *t.* David C. Rentz/Bruce Coleman; *b.* Rod Olanck/Tom Stack & Associates. 156: © Tom McHugh/Photo Researchers, Inc. 157: Silver Burdett. 160: Silver Burdett. 161: Edison National Historic Site.

Unit Three 164: E.R. Degginger. 164–165: Robert McKenzie/Tom Stack & Associates. 165: *l.* Fredrik D. Bodin/Stock, Boston; *r.* Frank Siteman/Stock, Boston.

Chapter 9 166–167: Grant Heilman Photography; 169: *l.* © Robert Bornemann/Photo Researchers, Inc.; *r.* Alan Pitcairn/Grant Heilman Photography. 170: Silver Burdett. 171: J.R. Eyerman/Black Star. 173: Ken Sakamoto/Black Star. 174–175: Grant Heilman Photography. 176: Clyde Smith/Peter Arnold, Inc. 177: *t.* © 1985 Nathan Benn/Woodfin Camp & Associates; *r.* Norman Tomalin/Bruce Coleman. 178: Silver Burdett. 179: *t.* Arnold Zann/Black Star; *b.* E.R. Degginger. 180: *t.* Phil Degginger; *b.* © Harald Sund. 181: *l.* Eric Carle /Shostal Associates; *r.* Jeffrey E. Blackman/The Stock Shop. 182: Grant Heilman Photography. 183: C.G Summers, Jr./Bruce Coleman.

Chapter 10 186–187: E.R. Degginger. 188: *t.* M. Vanderwall/Leo DeWys; *b.* Warren Dick/Shostal Associates. 189: Silver Burdett. 190: Victoria Beller-Smith for Silver Burdett. 191: *t.* Dick Garvey/West Stock; *b.* Phil Degginger. 192: Alan Pitcairn/Grant Heilman Photography. 193: *t.* Jose M. Rosario/Shostal Associates; *b.* © Longview Daily News 1980 by Roger Werth/Woodfin Camp & Associates. 194: Silver Burdett. 195: Jim Holland/Black Star. 196: *t.* Robert McKenzie/Tom Stack & Associates; *b.* Grant Heilman Photography. 197: *t.l.* © 1985 Martin Rodgers/Woodfin Camp & Associates; *t.l.* Silver Burdett; *t.r.* Laurent Maous/Gamma-Liaison. 198: Silver Burdett. 199: *l.* Frank Grant/International Stock Photo; *r.* E.R. Degginger. 200: *l.* Tom Tracy/Black Star. *r.* Nik Wheeler/Black Star. *r.* E.R. Degginger. Shop; *r.* E.R. Degginger. 201: *t.* © 1985 Michal Heron/Woodfin Camp & Associates; *b.r.* Hickson-Bender Photography for Silver Burdett; *t.r.* © Paolo Koch/Photo Researchers, Inc.

Chapter 11 204–205: © Tom McHugh/Photo Researchers. Inc. 206: George Rockwin/Bruce Coleman. 207: E.R. Degginger. 210: Victoria Beller-Smith for Silver Burdett. 211: *t.* Russ Kinne/Photo Researchers, Inc.; *b.* Tom Carroll/Alpha. 212: Cary Wolinsky/Stock, Boston. 213: *t.* John Curtis/Taurus Photos; *b.* © Lynn Hoffman/Photo Researchers, Inc. 214: *t.* Gary Milburn/Tom Stack & Associates; *m.* Michael P. Gadomski/Bruce Coleman; *b.* Victoria Beller-Smith for Silver Burdett. 215: *t.* Douglas Foulke/The Stock Shop; *m.* Ron Dillon/Tom Stack & Associates; *b.* B. Cory Kilvert, Jr./The Stock Shop. 216: Cary Wolinsky/Stock, Boston. 217: *t.* Runk/Schoenberger/Grant Heilman Photography; *t.r.* Clyde Smith/Peter Arnold, Inc; *b.r.* John Shaw/Tom Stack & Associates. 218: Grant Heilman Photography. 220: Silver Burdett.

Chapter 12 224–225: NASA. 226: Silver Burdett. 227: *l.* NASA; *r.* E.R. Degginger. 228: *t.* Tersch Enterprises; *b.* Silver Burdett; *b.* NASA. 231: Silver Burdett. 232–233: Tersch Enterprises. 234: Dan De Wilde for Silver Burdett. 235: Tersch Enterprises. 236, 238: Silver Burdett. 239: NASA. 242: *l.* Silver Burdett; *t.r.* L.L.T. Rhodes/Taurus Photos; *b.r.* NASA. 243: © Georg Gerster/Photo Researchers, Inc.

Unit Four 246: Michal Heron. 246–247: Medichrome/The Stock Shop. 247: *t.r.* Eric Fotran/Gartman Agency; *b.r.* Chuck Muhlstock/Focus on Sports.

Chapter 13 248–249: West Stock. 250–251: Imagery. 252: *t.* Imagery. *b.* Michal Heron. 253: Victoria Beller-Smith for Silver Burdett. 254–255: Copyright by the American Dental Association. Reprinted by Permission. 256: Michal Heron. 257: Jeffrey Reed/The Stock Shop. 258: *t.* Porges/Peter Arnold, Inc.; *b.* Dan De Wilde for Silver Burdett. 259: John Lei/Stock, Boston. 260: Silver Burdett. 261, 263: Dan De Wilde for Silver Burdett.

Chapter 14 266–267: Dan De Wilde for Silver Burdett. 268: *l.* Dan De Wilde for Silver Burdett; *r.* Elizabeth Crews/Stock, Boston. 269: Silver Burdett; except *b.l.* © George Leavens/Photo Researchers, Inc. 270: *t.* Focus on Sports; *b.* Silver Burdett. 271: *l., b.r.* Silver Burdett; *t.r.* Jeffry W. Myers/West Stock. 272: Dan De Wilde for Silver Burdett. 273: *l.* Dan De Wilde for Silver Burdett; *r.* Silver Burdett. 274: Victoria Beller-Smith for Silver Burdett. 275: Dan De Wilde for Silver Burdett. 276: Martha Cooper. 277: Silver Burdett. 278: Victoria Beller-Smith for Silver Burdett. 279: Silver Burdett. 280: Jacques Jangoux/Peter Arnold, Inc. 281: P. Schyler/Stock, Boston. 284: *l.* © Stephen Feldman/Photo Researchers, Inc.; *t.r.* Silver Burdett; *b.r.* Tom Tracy/Medichrome/The Stock Shop. 285: American Cancer Society